F.D.R. COLUMNIST

Franklin Roosevelt at Warm Springs

1924

F.D.R.
COLUMNIST

THE UNCOLLECTED COLUMNS
OF
FRANKLIN D. ROOSEVELT

FOREWORD BY ELEANOR ROOSEVELT
EDITED BY DONALD SCOTT CARMICHAEL

PELLEGRINI & CUDAHY ⁓⁓ CHICAGO

TO MARY GLENN

Foreword

MR. CARMICHAEL was a young friend of my husband. He collected these columns, written by my husband, and has asked me to write a foreword for them. I am very glad to do so.

In re-reading these columns which I had not read for many years, I was struck by the fact that my husband's interests had remained through the years attached to many of the same things, no matter how many new things were added. He cared about trees and woods and "lumber in general" all through his life, and on his own place, worked hard on an experimental basis with the Syracuse College of Forestry to improve his own land and his own woods.

I was more appreciative in re-reading these columns than I had been in the earlier days, of the way in which my husband managed to condense his information and write in a very short space, something really interesting and informative in each column. For instance, his interest in the improvement of the Civil Service was still with him up to the last year in Washington, and I do not think it will be divulging any secrets when I tell you that he had asked ex-Congressman Davenport, who had managed the Government interns program, to make a survey and recommend on how one could get new blood into the Civil Service and eliminate people who would be eliminated in ordinary business life. He appointed a committee and the report which is made on the reorganization of the government is still the best report that has been made on that subject, and is now being discussed in Congress and probably will be carried out in part.

My husband showed, in his columns, his interest in people and in living conditions, and he continued to work for people as the years went on. His devotion to his own part of the country never left him, no matter how much he traveled, nor how much he grew to be interested in other parts of the country.

He had a long training in politics and I think that was highly useful throughout his life, but the most useful of all was his background of country life and his ability to get joy and comfort out of the time spent in his own home surroundings. He always considered Hyde Park as home, no matter how long he lived in any other place.

ELEANOR ROOSEVELT

Val-Kill Cottage
Hyde Park, Dutchess County

TABLE OF CONTENTS

Columns in *The Standard,* Beacon, N. Y.:

ILLUSTRATIONS

F. D. R. COLUMNIST

INTRODUCTION

Mr. Roosevelt and the Press

THIS BOOK is a collection of the newspaper columns which Franklin Roosevelt wrote at Warm Springs as a substitute columnist for the Macon (Georgia) *Daily Telegraph* in 1925 and at Hyde Park for the Beacon (New York) *Standard* in 1928. It adds no world-shaking conclusions for the historians of Mr. Roosevelt's role in the era which bears his name. In the panorama of recent American history which the figure of Mr. Roosevelt dominates, this little collection is only a detail, a focus upon a few slight lines in the background. But it has seemed worth the trouble of unearthing and preserving precisely because of that— precisely because it presents a miniature of the late President in the years when he was recovering from infantile paralysis and again beginning to articulate his political ideas.

It seemed to present, also, a very human miniature; a picture of the future President in a minor role for which he had a boyish fondness. In the midst of his world-wide responsibility in his later years, he took delight in reminding newspapermen that he once edited the Harvard *Crimson*. He enjoyed the atmosphere of the easy-going fellowship of the press. He loved the give and take of his press conferences, was proud of his ability to joust with reporters in the terms of their trade. He liked newspapermen and as a class they liked him. He enjoyed his position among them. It was not simply that his administration furnished what was surely the most exciting series of newspaper stories in history. With his sense of a good story and his extraordinary gift for phrase-making, FDR had a way of pointing up the drama of what was happening, timing it, and fixing it forever in a phrase that simply had to be a headline. When a well-known newspaperman was asked what columnist he regarded as the most influential, he said that was easy: "Franklin Delano Roosevelt. He can hit the front page with a column of his own opinions any day he wants to. And we've got to print it. Those other guys (Dorothy Thompson, Winchell, Pearson, Mark Sullivan, Lippmann and Pegler) are inside right next to our editorials, where they could do the most harm, and we can drop them—and do—whenever we feel like it. But you've got to run FDR—that or quit trying to run a newspaper." The magnetism was reciprocal: Arthur Krock called Mr. Roosevelt "the greatest reader and critic of newspapers . . . ever seen in the Presidential office."

In a small way, it completes the picture to see FDR himself in two brief terms as a newspaperman, the first time as a convalescent in Warm Springs "whitewashing a fence for Tom Loyless" and the second time at his family home in Hyde Park, at the outset of Al Smith's Presidential campaign, with national issues looming over the chatty column he called "Between Neighbors."

THE GOOD NEIGHBOR

IN WARM SPRINGS

The Good Neighbor
In Warm Springs

THE BACKGROUND of Mr. Roosevelt's brief newspaper stint
in Warm Springs was his affectionate friendship for Tom Loyless,
one of Georgia's outstanding newspapermen and a pioneer in the
development of Warm Springs.

It was a friendship that developed in the quiet days of convalescence, when Mr. Roosevelt had the cottage of Leighton Mac-
Pherson, a few doors from the Loyless cottage. At that time, FDR
was accompanied only by his secretary, Marguerite LeHand, and
a husky Negro valet. Members of the Loyless family recall Mr.
Roosevelt's hearty appetite for companionship, how he sometimes
complained that the Loylesses did not come over to his cottage
often enough. He would roll himself out on the porch and call,
"Come on over." Whoever was at home in the Loyless cottage
would go over for a visit.

One day FDR asked several people, most of them friends or
relatives of Tom Loyless, to a cocktail party. America was still
in the very depths of Prohibition and so the affair was fairly hush-
hush. Roosevelt was in a very jovial mood for his guests and he
soon had Loyless engaged in their favorite sport of fast exchange,
topping each other's story and sending off sparks of repartee.

Everybody was soon in it and the atmosphere was one pandemonium of laughter. Tom Loyless' sister and Miss LeHand were in the kitchen mixing cocktails, and as one of the ladies was bringing in a tray of drinks, there was a knock at the door. Miss LeHand went to it with gay confidence and nonchalance and found herself suddenly confronted with the local Baptist preacher. The cocktails were quickly covered with an apron and returned to the kitchen. FDR sat there agonized with laughter.

It was Loyless who had first interested Mr. Roosevelt in giving his aid and confidence to Warm Springs as a center for the after-treatment of infantile paralysis. Loyless had come to his position as lessee manager of Warm Springs by a circuitous route. Loyless was born in Dawson, Terrell County, Georgia, in 1870. He became an orphan at an early age, and his schooling was meager. With his instinct for news, he drifted into the newspaper business. As a boy he wrote up the parties and other doings which he attended and he took such items to the Dawson *News* for publication. At the age of 17, he was an apprentice staff reporter for that paper and fitted himself for the larger field he entered upon going to Macon. Between 1887 and 1895 he successively served as staff reporter for the Macon *News,* city editor for the Macon *Daily Telegraph* and managing editor and part owner of the Knoxville *Sentinel.* He was editor and publisher of the Macon *News* from 1895 to 1899. For the next four years he continued his newspaper work in Atlanta, first as assistant editor of the Atlanta *Journal,* then as an associate of the elder Clark Howell of the Atlanta *Constitution.* For the sixteen years between 1903 and 1919, Loyless was editor and publisher of the Augusta *Chronicle,* "the South's oldest newspaper." At the time he acquired the *Chronicle* it was in receivership, and under Loyless' aegis it became one of the most widely respected of Georgia's dailies.

Loyless' hatred of intolerance brought forth a fierce anger which evoked some of his most brilliant writing. Typical of such writing are the editorials he wrote for the *Chronicle* at the time of the Leo Frank lynchings and during his long fight against the late Senator Tom Watson, Georgia's brilliant rabble-rouser. The *Chronicle* is said to have been largely responsible for Watson's publication being barred from the mails for his obscene attacks on Catholics and Jews. Loyless was recognized as one of the best political writers in the South—absolutely fearless, personally and professionally.

In the fall of 1919, Loyless sold his interest in the *Chronicle* and associated himself with Julian Harris, son of Joel Chandler Harris (of "Uncle Remus" fame) in the ownership of the *Enquirer-Sun* at Columbus, Georgia. He served as editor of the paper; his partner as business manager. Loyless refused, as always, to mix the business policy of the paper with its editorial policy. As editor, he waged an uphill fight against the Ku Klux Klan. At the time he fought the Klan it was dangerous, not only politically and financially, but personally as well; yet he made the Klan fight a policy of the *Enquirer-Sun* despite the fact that it was ruinous to advertising revenue. Many Southerners insist that his long and successful battle led to the eventual dissolution of that organization. Julian Harris received the Pulitzer prize for journalism for this achievement, but those who knew more of the story behind the *Enquirer-Sun's* policy felt that the prize should have gone to Tom Loyless posthumously. There is little doubt that he was the architect of that policy. It was over this very issue and the effect of the *Enquirer-Sun's* editorial policy on advertising income that Harris and Loyless parted ways in November 1922. On November 18, the *Enquirer-Sun* carried a statement giving Loyless' reasons for his resignation as president and editor of the paper. This statement Loyless offered "herewith in lieu of an editorial which I had

7

prepared for publication Sunday, but about which Mr. Julian Harris and I have irrevocably differed." Loyless declared that for twenty-eight years his editorial pen had been "free and untrammeled" and that for the time left him he was determined that it should remain so. This was the end of Loyless' career as an active newspaperman.

But the effects of newsprint and printer's ink on one's corpuscles are not so easily disowned. During a state political campaign in Georgia, he became a columnist for a paper he had worked on in the early days. Commencing in the summer of 1924, the Macon *Daily Telegraph* ran his column "As Loyless Sees It," every other day on its editorial page.

Meanwhile Warm Springs had already impressed itself as an element in Loyless' life. As a boy he spent summers at Warm Springs with his family. In later years he often vacationed there. Charles Davis, who owned the resort for many years, was a friend dating back to the family summers there. In approximately 1920 Loyless developed a business interest in Warm Springs. He organized the Warm Springs Operating Company to run it on a lease. This company was a family affair composed of Mr. and Mrs. Loyless and Mrs. Loyless' three brothers. The little group ran the place as a pleasure resort with the large public pool of warm, invigorating, spring water as the main attraction. This watering place had long attracted those people who wished to take advantage of the baths for health purposes, but when sufferers from infantile paralysis showed new strength after swimming there, Tom Loyless envisioned the improvement of the property as a health center. However, his group did not have the money to finance the project on the scale necessary to succeed. He interested others, therefore, in putting money in a successor corporation known as the Georgia Warm Springs Company. The company then obtained a five year option to purchase the property from Miss Georgia Wilkins, a niece who had inherited the property from Mr. Davis upon his death in the early 1920's. Loyless also interested a fellow-Georgian, George Foster Peabody, in acquiring a half interest in the resort property. Hence the ownership became joint, and the Loyless group operated the property.

It was on behalf of the Warm Springs project that Tom Loyless met Mr. Roosevelt for the first time. The meeting was probably arranged by Peabody, who was an old friend of FDR. It was logical for those interested in the rejuvenation of Warm Springs to seek Roosevelt's interest. He could be of immeasurable help in the promotion. He had money, could attract money, and was himself a sufferer from infantile paralysis. It was undoubtedly with this in mind that Loyless visited Mr. Roosevelt in New York.

Knowing enough about hydrotherapy to put some measure of credence in what Loyless told him about Warm Springs, FDR determined to investigate for himself. On several occasions since, usually in talking with his young friends and neighbors at the annual Warm Springs Thanksgiving dinners, Roosevelt described his arrival there:

> I remember a September of 1924, when I turned up here and occupied the only cottage, with one exception, that was open. The hotel was closed. Everything was closed and almost everything was falling to pieces. Most of the roofs leaked . . .
> It was a perfectly good down-at-the-heel summer resort and nothing else. . . . It was in awful condition.
> The only people who were here when we arrived were Mr. and Mrs. Loyless and old Mr. Watts, the postman. . . . When we came down, there was no doctor around here; there was nobody in charge, or anything of a medical nature. I went down to what is now the public pool. It was rather simple in those days. . . .

Mr. Roosevelt's recollections of the general situation at Warm Springs are pretty accurate, but apparently a bit hazy on details. As a matter of fact, besides Mr. and Mrs. Loyless and the postman, there was William Kennedy, brother-in-law of Loyless and manager of the pool which was the chief source of income of the Warm Springs company. Kennedy recalls that he was winding up the summer's business at the time of FDR's first visit. He also recalls FDR's first swim in the pool and the fact that there were several cottages at the resort still open because the Indian summer was particularly beautiful that year.

In any case, the dilapidated condition of the resort was apparently of no great consequence to Franklin Roosevelt. On October 14, 1924, he said in a letter to his friend Peabody:

> . . . Every morning I spend two hours in the most wonderful pool in the world, and it is no exaggeration to say that the muscles in my legs have improved to an extent noticeable in every way. I have had many talks with Mr. Loyless about the development of the property. There is no question that in the average case of infantile paralysis this Warm Springs pool is a great find . . .

Besides the hospitality of Tom Loyless, another friendship made Warm Springs a neighborly place for FDR on the occasion of that first visit. At the long, drawn out Democratic National Convention of 1924 in New York Mr. Roosevelt had been floor manager for Alfred E. Smith. There he met Major John S. Cohen of the Atlanta *Journal,* who was a leader of the McAdoo forces. Despite their desire to see different men win the Democratic leadership, Major Cohen and FDR became good friends. During recesses in the convention they often conversed at the Hotel Pennsylvania.

FDR mentioned his interest in Warm Springs, about which he had learned from Loyless, and Major Cohen urged Mr. Roosevelt to come to Georgia as his guest and visit Warm Springs. At the time of Mr. Roosevelt's first visit, Major Cohen was ill and sent a political writer for the *Journal* named Cleburne E. Gregory to Warm Springs to be of any service possible to the visitor. Gregory recalls Mr. Roosevelt's visit in a letter to the present writer:

> I went swimming in Warm Springs with Mr. Roosevelt two or three times a day for five days. We ate hot dogs at a small, unsanitary stand adjacent to the pool and washed them down with an occasional bottle of beer.
> Mr. Roosevelt laughed at the claims of the Cherokee Indians that the springs had medicinal value, but he said the water's temperature of 89 degrees soothed muscles drawn by infantile paralysis and encouraged mild exercise. I wrote a story about his visit for the *Journal* Sunday Magazine with the title: "Roosevelt Is Swimming His Way Back to Health."

Mr. Gregory's story originally appeared in the Sunday Magazine of the Atlanta *Journal,* October 26, 1924. The exact title was "Franklin Roosevelt Will Swim to Health." Roosevelt was pictured swimming in the pool, sun bathing, and in an informal pose as he appeared at that time. His falling victim to infantile paralysis, how he came to visit the Georgia resort, and the help he found there, were all recounted. The newspaper story stated that FDR "is literally swimming himself back to health. Mr. Roosevelt does not know how he contracted the dread disease, and does not regard himself as more outstanding or unfortunate than the hundreds of other adults who became victims at the same time by the disease usually confined to childhood." Gregory went on to say that the visitor "has the large swimming pool all to himself for two hours or more each day. He swims, dives, uses the swinging rings and horizontal bar over the water, and finally crawls out on the concrete pier for a sun bath that lasts another hour." The reporter continued, saying that after dressing and having lunch, Roosevelt "rests a bit on a delightfully shady porch, and spends the afternoon driving over the surrounding country, in which he is intensely interested." In conclusion, Gregory observed:

Mr. Roosevelt has made a great hit with the people of Warm Springs who have met him, and they are extending him a hearty welcome as a prospective regular visitor. A number of Georgia's public men have also called to pay their respects and extend greetings. Georgians who attended the Democratic national convention have been especially cordial, because they appreciate the interest Mr. Roosevelt showed in them, and his courtesy in apologizing, as an Al Smith leader, for unfortunate and embarrassing incidents in connection with the convention.

"Say! Let's get one of the hot dogs this man makes just outside the swimming pool. They're great," Mr. Roosevelt challenged. With him everything in Warm Springs is "Great" or "Fine" or "Wonderful." That is the spirit that has carried him to remarkable heights for a man just past his fortieth year, and it is the spirit that is going to restore him to his pristine health and vigor, for political and financial battles and successes in the years that are to come.

It is interesting to note than in 1940, when Mr. Roosevelt was considering a third term, he called a number of Georgia political leaders to Warm Springs for a conference which was attended by Gregory. It so happened that this political writer was the only one who could answer some of the President's questions about Georgia's politics. When Gregory spoke out in the meeting FDR reportedly looked at him quizzically and puzzled over him during the rest of the conference. As the group began to leave the cottage, the President is said to have called him back and remarked: "Gregory, haven't you and I been on a junket somewhere together?" The newspaperman replied that he was flattered the President remembered—that he had helped to welcome FDR to Warm Springs. "Of course," Mr. Roosevelt replied. "Didn't we have a good time in the springs and weren't those hot dogs good?"

Refreshed and encouraged by his progress at Warm Springs, FDR was back in New York early in November 1924. There he undertook in an active way to harmonize and unite the Democratic Party nationally. The defeat of the Democratic ticket in 1920 and the national convention of the party in 1924 with all its factional strife—Bryan supporting McAdoo against Smith, the South and West against the East, the Klan versus Catholicism—all but wrecked the party of Woodrow Wilson. One of the few bright interludes in that bitter struggle was Roosevelt's dramatic nomination of Al Smith at the convention. The "Happy Warrior" speech is now famous. Franklin Roosevelt came out of the convention increased in stature. On July 7, 1924, during those events, the New York *Evening World* observed:

> Franklin D. Roosevelt stands out as the real hero of the Democratic Convention of 1924.
> Adversity has lifted him above the bickering, the religious bigotry, conflicting personal ambitions and petty sectional prejudices. It has made him the one leader commanding the respect and admiration of delegations from all sections of the land . . . Roosevelt might be a pathetic, tragic figure but for the fine courage that flashes in his smile. It holds observers enchained.
> . . . The delegates to this convention, if permitted to

break the deadlock in their own way, undoubtedly would vote for Franklin D. Roosevelt, with the red badge of courage pinned to his breast.

An acknowledged leader in the party, Mr. Roosevelt wrote to more than a thousand Democratic leaders throughout the country including the delegates to the party convention in the previous June. His letter, written in December 1924, asked their counsel on the best means of "making the Democracy stronger and more militant nationally." The responses received moved him, in February 1925, to suggest to Senator Thomas J. Walsh of Montana that a national conference of Democratic leaders be called. The purpose of such a meeting was to be the revitalization of the party and the taking of "common counsel." The leaders whom he had written, he said, "were overwhelmingly agreed that the Democracy must be unqualifiedly the party representative of progress and liberal thought" and that "the Democracy must make it clear that it seeks primarily the good of the average citizen through the free rule of the whole electorate, as opposed to the Republican party, which seeks a mere moneyed prosperity of the nation, through the control of Government by a self-appointed aristocracy of wealth and social and economic power."

The leaders he called upon were, according to Mr. Roosevelt, "insistent that the Democratic party shall not, nationally, in the future confuse with basic principles those matters of momentary or temporary nature which are principally of local interest. By thus confining itself to those issues which the whole party, in every section of the nation, agrees on as fundamental, we shall not only present a united front, but shall cease to confuse the electorate."

In replying and expressing himself "in entire harmony" with the proposal for a conference to bind up the party wounds and develop common purpose, Senator Walsh found the views expressed by Mr. Roosevelt and the delegates bore "a remarkable similarity" to opinions he had received from many Democrats solicitous about the party's future.

The New York *Times,* March 10, 1925, welcomed FDR's plan:

"Any rational plan for smoothing out the factional animosities that, with other causes, brought so signal a disaster upon the Democratic Party last year deserves welcome and encouragement. The correspondence between Mr. Franklin D. Roosevelt and Senator Walsh of Montana discloses such a plan . . ."

However, FDR's efforts to get the Democratic leaders together in a harmony conference were not successful. The New York *Times* said editorially on April 10, 1925: "Mr. Franklin D. Roosevelt's well-meant proposal for a harmony meeting of Democrats, though kindly received by Senator Walsh of Montana, has gone glimmering. A conference of Democrats to discuss party reorganization could only result in greater disorganization so long as the Democratic Party is divided into factions. These factions, in part sectional, represent not only opposite policies, but rival leaders. The bitterness and disappointment of 1924 have not had time to cool. . ."

In the early spring of 1925 Franklin Roosevelt went south, as was his custom, to cruise and fish off the Florida coast, planning to follow this with a second visit to Warm Springs.

The winter at Warm Springs had been a hard one for Tom Loyless. His health was failing, and he had spent the winter months trying to renovate the resort so that the prospective patients, resulting from Gregory's story of FDR's improvement, could be handled. The correspondence between FDR and TWL in that period runs like this:

Loyless wrote to Roosevelt:

> I have neuritis and am in low ground of sorrow. Your visit certainly put Warm Springs on the map—as Taft's visit did Augusta. With this neuritis hold of me, or whatever it is, I welcome a little sunshine; for, as the drunken fellow said as he rolled out of the street into the gutter, to get out of the way of a runaway team, "I am in no condition to be run-over."

Three months later he wrote to Roosevelt:

> I think I have moved nearly everything in the Warm Springs premises within the past six weeks, except the springs themselves and a few pine trees. Our first patient showed up, from Birmingham. He seemed pretty well-to-do; at least he came in a Lincoln car—and that always spells money to me. I am unable to do anything at all for him at present.

On March tenth:

> I broke the "e" on my typewriter, pounding out my articles for the *Telegraph,* so that I have been able to write only for the printer and to my wife. They will stand for almost anything from me. A bit tired but I enjoy it, all except my experience, for the past week or more, with a booze-fighting house-mover. Have been having five or six of the hotel cottages moved around a bit—and the man I gave the contract to has been drunk [sic] soon after he got started. I must say I can't much blame him, but it is hard on me, as I never know where he is going to take the next one—and I don't think he does. I have tried some stunts myself, in days past, with more or less liquor in me, but I never tried to move houses.

And as to Roosevelt's return to Warm Springs in April, 1925:

> The Southern train for Warm Springs leaves Columbus
> at 3:25 but I might arrange to have it held for you—as I
> don't think I would inconvenience anyone, except the con-
> ductor and engineer, if I did.

Mr. Roosevelt arrived for his second visit to Warm Springs
early in April. Continuing his swimming and treatment in the
pool, he also pitched in to help Tom with the patients who were
now beginning to arrive at the as yet unprepared health center.
The situation that spring has been described by Mr. Roosevelt:

> One day Mr. Loyless and some of the neighbors—the
> Harts, Miss Wilkins and Josephs and some of us—were
> sitting around when a messenger came up the hill to Mr.
> Loyless and said, "Two people have been carried off the
> train down at the station. What shall we do with them?
> Neither of them can walk."
> Well, we held a consultation. It was long before any-
> thing was done here in the way of a hotel or cottages. We
> decided that we could take care of them in the village over-
> night, and then, in a couple of days, we could fix up what
> is now "The Wreck," and put them in it. Well, before
> we could put that cottage in order, eight others had arrived.
> They came like Topsy and got here before we knew it.
> We did not know what to do with them so I sent for
> Dr. Johnson. He came and looked them over and guar-
> anteed that they did not have heart trouble or something
> from which they would suddenly die, and he recommended
> cream and fattening diets for some and he recommended
> very little food for some of the others.
> And then I undertook to be doctor and physiotherapist,
> all rolled into one. I taught Fred Botts to swim. I taught
> them all at least to play around in the water. I remember
> there were two quite large ladies; and when I was trying

to teach them an exercise I had really invented, which was the elevating exercise in the medium of water, one of these ladies found great difficulty in getting both feet down to the bottom of the pool. Well I would take one large knee and I would force this large knee and leg down until the foot rested firmly on the bottom. And then I would say, "Have you got it?" and she would say, "Yes," and I would say, "Hold it, hold it." Then I would reach up and get hold of the other knee very quickly and start to put it down and then number one knee would pop up. This used to go on for half an hour at a time; but before I left in the spring, I would get both knees down at the same time.

This, then, was the setting in which Tom Loyless called on his "good neighborman" Franklin Roosevelt to take over his job with the *Daily Telegraph*. Tom was tired—more tired than he knew—and his April 14th column announced that there would be a substitute. In that column, in his characteristic homely style, Loyless gives us a precious record of that setting. Through Franklin Roosevelt, Tom Loyless was close to great history, and somehow, beneath the gentle kidding, we see that he knew it. Here, in that April 14th column, is Franklin Roosevelt as the good neighbor in Warm Springs, himself an invalid, but insisting with boyish earnestness that his best use toward helping Tom get a rest would be in taking over the road-building job at the resort. That earnestness for the small things and small people at Warm Springs—most of the sufferers were children—was to continue through an inhumanly busy lifetime. Here, too, is the future world-statesman regaining his strength and using every new ounce of it to rally his party to reorganize and rebuild into something strong, liberal, and truly national. Tom Loyless saw that too, and took the trouble and the space to print in full the letters which FDR was sending in every direction to party-leaders. One letter begins: "I am taking the baths at Warm Springs, Ga., in an effort to get rid of my crutches. If it were not for that I would be with you at your Jefferson Day Dinner." Franklin Roosevelt was regaining his strength and was seeing, more and more clearly, what he meant to use this strength for. Tom Loyless gives us this whole scene so well that his long column is worth having in its entirety:

Unless all signs fail, this will be about the last you will see of this column, as such—under its present caption, at least—for some days, and I hope weeks, to come.

For truth to tell, I have about made arrangements to do the "Tom Sawyer act" and let somebody else whitewash my fence for awhile. That is, if I can get the other party to the agreement to sign up; and, also, get the editor's consent to the arrangement—about which latter, I haven't the slightest doubt. For he has too much sense not to jump at that sort of "exchange" when he gets the chance—or else he's fooled me all along, these thirty-odd years past.

And, as for The Telegraph's hundred thousand or so readers—I have forgotten just exactly the number Peyt Anderson told me the last time—they will owe me a vote of thanks for once, if never before, or again.

Well, it is like this: The other night I was over at a neighbor's house—Dr. McCallie, the State Geologist, being over there "visiting" with me—right across our Cherokee rose fence, just sitting around talking geology and balneology and one thing and another, when my neighbor said I looked "tired" and "all rundown," and that I "ought to take a rest," and all that sort of thing.

"What with trying to direct and keep up with two or three carpenter gangs, and plumbers and roofers and painters and paper hangers and concrete workers and electricians and pipefitters and pump installers, road-builders, I am afraid you are overdoing it a bit, and you will have to let up for a little," this good neighbor went on.

Also, he said, that if I would turn a part of our working force over to him—preferably our road-building gang—

he would get in his car and look after the road work for me from day to day while he is down here. And, by way of self recommendation, he frankly admitted that he was a sort of "shark" at road-building; that he had built a lot of roads, in his youth and since, whenever the notion struck him, on the family estate, at Hyde Park, up on the Hudson, etc., etc.

All of which, of course, touched me deeply—but not enough for me to take my chances with my road work. So, I told this good neighborman, that if he wanted to be a real help to me in my present run-down condition, as well as lighten the load on my mind and conscience, there was still another division of labor that would take a much bigger load off of me than mere road building—which, when you come right down to it, ought to be a pleasure and a recreation for any out-door man.

"Let's have it," he said, "anything to save a life."

And, then I told him—breaking it as gently to him as I could, of course.

"Do my stuff on The Macon Telegraph for me for a few days," I suggested, "and heaven, as well as I and the general public, will bless you."

"But why not the road work, instead?" he countered. "Evidently you have never seen any of my road work."

I have not, and I admitted it. But I also admitted that he didn't look like a road-builder. Further, that I had to be just a bit particular with our roads around Warm Springs, but that it didn't matter so much what goes on in my column—as any reader of The Telegraph will attest.

"That being the case," he replied, "and with the proviso that Editor Anderson will stand for it, I will, here and now, agree to write your column for you for a few times— until you can rest up and get your brain properly functioning again, if it ever does, assuming, of course, that the editor will allow me as much latitude as he does you— which is a lot more than I would allow either of us if I were in his place."

So, that's where we left it—until we can put it up to the editor and see what he has to say about it. But if he doesn't grab the proposition, he hasn't the sense that, for some reason or other, I have always credited him with having.

However, I wish to have this distinctly understood in advance—particularly with "P. T." and the business office—that no matter who "whitewashes my fence" for me, I draw the pay for it, such as it is.

This being perfectly understood and agreed upon in writing in advance, I may pull down my sign for a few days, or as long as I can get my neighbors to "sub" for me, and put in its place, "As Roosevelt Sees It"—for, of course, you knew who I was talking about all the time.

Even in advance of all that, however, I have asked him to let me print in The Telegraph some of those "Jefferson Day" letters and telegrams he has been sending out from here these past few days—declining to speak at Jefferson Day dinners here, there and yonder. As if any normal Democrat could be "hongry" enough to hanker for that sort of job right now.

Well, anyway, asking you and his pardon for the seeming levity of what has gone before; which is caused only by the prospect of having someone, particularly SUCH a someone, do my stuff for me for awhile free of charge anyway. I say, here are some of the letters that Hon. Franklin D. Roosevelt has sent out to a few, more or less, Democratic strongholds within the past few days; all of which make good reading, whether you believe Al Smith is a secret agent of the Pope, or that McAdoo still has oil on him:

At Warm Springs, Ga., April 8, 1925

To the Young Men's Democratic Club
Kansas City, Mo.

I am taking the baths at Warm Springs, Ga., in an effort to get rid of my crutches. If it were not for this I would be with you at your Jefferson Day Dinner.

May I emphasize to you a fundamental, essentially American fact? The Democratic party must, for the good of the nation, be ever viewed as a national party. It is, today, in the millions of men and women in its ranks, the representative of liberal and progressive thought. This is true in the East and the South, as well as in the West. We will always have with us men and women who are more reactionary or more radical than the rank and file, and we will always have with us leaders who seek to advance their personal future at the expense of the national character of the party itself. Sectional blindness or personal selfishness can delay but never permanently crush our ultimate national success!

This is the time for unselfishness and for what Woodrow Wilson called common counsel. Existing differences between Democrats are in large part over what should be considered properly as local issues. As one who has the privilege of knowing every State in the Union, I venture the assertion that the rank and file of Democrats in every State are in substantial agreement on the national principles of the Republican party.

It is not enough to wait for thieves to fall out among themselves in the halls of Congress or the departments of the government—it is not enough to wait until Republicans present us with another scandal—the issues are here today. Government by Republican leaders is openly government by privilege.

It is time for the Democracy to drop opportunism, to organize for militant action and to restate the fundamentals in which we all believe. A few ounces of unselfishness and of common counsel at this time will be worth many tons of speech-making and costly effort at a later date.

Very sincerely yours,

FRANKLIN D. ROOSEVELT

At Warm Springs, Ga., April 8, 1925

Hon. Joseph F. Guffey, Pittsburgh, Pa.

My dear Mr. Guffey:

I have only just received your telegram down here in the South. I very much regret that I cannot go to the

Jefferson Day Dinner of the Democracy of Western Pennsylvania.

I trust and believe that soon we shall have a greater degree of common counsel and of militant organization within our party. It is time for unselfishness and for the elimination of personalities. I note that by far the largest part of the publicity which describes Democratic discord comes from easily traceable Republican organization sources. An overwhelming conservative press serves them as a willing, though sometimes unconscious, tool.

The way to organize is to organize—and the way to get together is to meet together!

Very sincerely yours,

FRANKLIN D. ROOSEVELT

At Warm Springs, Ga., April 9, 1925

To the Members of the National League of
Progressive Democracy:

I had a long talk last week with Mr. William Jennings Bryan at Miami and I wish we could both be at the banquet in Washington on April 13. There appears to be every reason for Democrats throughout the country to take common counsel at this time. The rank and file of the party in every section of the country endorse the same basic principles. It is, of course, perfectly obvious that the well organized machinery of the Republicans, including the vast majority of the large newspapers, is painting lurid pictures of Democratic discord. As a matter of simple fact most of this so-called discord relates to local or personal matters as distinguished from national principles. The Republican party has within its rank and file more true discord in that they differ among themselves on matters of basic principle.

I might add that opportunism will never bring us victory. It is bad gospel to preach that we should wait with our hands folded until the Republicans once more, in their administration or in their Congress, lay themselves

23

open to attack through some new scandal or family row. The issue recurs in every act of those who control the Republican party. They, flushed with success, openly admit their sole idea to be that of prosperity—the prosperity of money and yet more money—a materialism for the immediate benefit of the privileged few, but colored with the deliberate objective of deceiving the average citizen into the erroneous belief that it will benefit the many.

With the old American fundamental thought of honest government for the benefit of the many, the Republican leaders have no sympathy.

Through the elimination of personalities, through the laying aside of personal ambitions, through the perfecting of organization and, finally, through an honest effort on the part of every section in the nation to talk things over and get together, the Democracy can, today, lay the foundation for a successful appeal to the confidence of the electorate.

FRANKLIN D. ROOSEVELT

Thus Franklin Roosevelt took on Tom's job. And after he had written the column under the caption *Roosevelt Says* for several days and completed his stay at Warm Springs, FDR again went North. The Tom Loyless whom he left at Warm Springs was a very sick man, and an operation in August, 1925, proved he had cancer. After the operation he returned to Warm Springs, but as the cottages were poorly equipped for cold weather, Mrs. Loyless took him to his daughter's home in Pennsylvania. About this time Tom wrote a letter, a copy of which he sent Mr. Roosevelt. Despair had come over him:

I have made mistakes, errors of judgment, miscalculations, etc. etc. Some of them are my fault outright, some, possibly, the fault of others, though I recognize my own responsibility even for that, and some of it is nobody's fault at all. I, it seems, who had to plan it all and execute it,

24

even to the point of undermining my health, and piling up a doctor's bill and a drug bill of several hundred dollars, and a board bill with Mrs. B. of like account must "forage for myself." In the meantime I have had to give up my Macon *Telegraph* work, on account of my physical condition, and my last life insurance policy, on account of my financial condition, and I have now nothing left I can give up to it, except possibly my life.

It would appear that despite his suffering, his sheer will-power and desire to see his dream for Warm Springs come true enabled Loyless to live on. His daughter once told the present writer in a letter how FDR had helped to buoy him up:

> One of our greatest causes for gratitude to Mr. Roosevelt was the manner in which, in accordance with the doctor's wishes, he joined with us in the pretense that Daddy's complete recovery was just a matter of time. My mother had of course told him (Mr. R.) from the beginning that he had cancer but all letters from him were so full of plans that they gave Daddy an intense interest in life and kept him from giving way to despair.

Despite the doctors' prediction that Loyless could not live more than two months after the operation, he lived until March 21, 1926. FDR was cruising off the Florida coast when he heard the news of the death of Tom Loyless, and he wrote the following letter from the Houseboat *Larooco:*

> My dear Mrs. Loyless:
> The very sad news has only just come down here among the Florida Keys. It is a shock in so many ways—but more than all I feel that I have lost one of my really best friends. Somehow from the very first day he came into my office in N. Y. even before my first visit to Warm Springs I had that feeling of deep and sincere friendship and you know how it ripened when we were living "across the way."

Somehow since last Spring I had grown so accustomed to the thought of his illness that I couldn't bring myself to realize that I would not be able to see him this Spring—I don't think I have ever known anyone who had a keener *soul* than T.W.L.—not just his brilliant mind, but the deeper fundamentals of right and wrong in his whole being —and his fine courage too deserved many many more years of service.

I am going to dear old Warm Springs Mar. 28 and as you know have been negotiating with the Peabodys for many weeks, but it is not settled yet. In any event your good husband's spirit will always dispense goodness and help to the many who will some day see his dream come true.

I hope much that you may be there in April while I am still there—

Faithfully yours,
FRANKLIN D. ROOSEVELT

We all know that Franklin Roosevelt went on to risk a large part of his personal fortune to purchase the old resort and establish Georgia Warm Springs Foundation, bringing to fruition Tom Loyless' dream that the crippled could be helped to walk again if given access to these waters. Franklin Roosevelt went on—went on to Albany and Washington, to Placentia Bay and Casablanca, to Quebec, Teheran and Yalta—then back to his white cottage on Pine Mountain where he had gone so often for new strength of body and soul during those twenty years of great action. It was there at Warm Springs, where he and Tom Loyless had come to know each other well, where they had planned together a center of hope and courage for the victims of a demoralizing sickness, where FDR had whitewashed Tom's fence for him—it was there he was on that beautiful spring day when the azaleas were in bloom again—April 12, 1945.

COLUMNS

IN

THE MACON DAILY TELEGRAPH

1925

OUR EDUCATIONAL PROBLEMS

The educators who are meeting here today have one great common thought: that doubtless all their activities. They are looking for the best way out of the quagmire that has bogged the State and impeded her march toward progress. They are seeking the best method of improving the educational system of our State.

They have a tremendous task, but they have undertaken it with a singular oneness of purpose. Although we have a compulsory education law, only seven out of ten children of school age attend school; in eighty-eight counties of this State, so more than half the counties—something more than 135,000 white children who attend school, but to mention the 16,000 in those counties who should be in school, but are not, have six months or less of schooling during the year. The latest available statistics on illiteracy indicate that there are 249,000 illiterates out of our total population of approximately 2,900,000 persons.

WHAT ONE MAN DID

AFRAID TO BE PROGRESSIVE

BETTING ON A "CINCH"

IN THE NECK, AS USUAL

JUST TWIXT US
By BRIDGES SMITH

A GOOD MORNING TO YOU
A Verse and a Vignette
By D. C. BICKERS

THIS MONTH.

ROOSEVELT SAYS:

LETTERS TO

Roosevelt's First Column in *The Macon Daily Telegraph*

April 16, 1925

I

"I Have Returned to My Former Profession"

Thursday, April 16, 1925

I HAVE TO take off my hat to still another product of Georgia—its newspaper men.

Here am I over at Warm Springs, an expert road builder, all ready, with my coat off, to lay out and construct miles of beautifully graded, guaranteed not-to-wash-out, paths through the azalea-covered woods of Pine Mountain, while Tom Loyless sits with his feet up in his cottage, across the street, writing diatribes for The Telegraph.

But I knew I would be double-crossed—I always do [sic] by these newspaper men. He now is out picking wild flowers and I have returned to my former profession—I used to edit the college paper in the old days.

He did it to me once before. Last Autumn I was swimming in the Warm Springs Pool, and T.W.L. sauntered by and introduced a delightful youngster to me. Never mind his name. I thought he was a mere cousin or something of that sort. We talked about health and crops and politics and soon thereafter I went back home to Dutchess County, New York. Then came the newspaper clippings—whole sheets of them—Sunday supplements, illustrations—from every paper between here and Seattle, Wash. There I was, large as life, living proof that Warm Springs, Georgia, had cured me of 57 different varieties of ailments. Most of the diseases from which I had suffered were apparently fatal, but Warm Springs evidently had got each just in time, giving me a chance to go out and catch another incurable malady and dash back here to get rid of it. That enterprising youngster who syndicated the article must have made several fortunes out of it, but he never even sent me a 5 per cent commission.

Worse than that—it started a flood of correspondence, which hasn't reached its crest yet. I thought I had a good many people writing me letters before that, but since last November I have had to take on six or eight additional secretaries and stenographers to handle my mail. Every human being, male or female, between Florida and Alaska who has a stomach-ache, a cold in the nose or a gouty toe, it would seem, writes to old Dr. Roosevelt, with the firm belief that I can point out to them, from personal experience, how to get cured. Why, they are going to raise my little postoffice up on the Hudson River from a third-class office to a first-class office because of the increased number of stamps I have had to buy (no longer having the privilege of using "official business" envelopes of our Uncle Sam for nothing). It sure is time to get another Democratic administration; maybe, then, I can get the franking privilege back.

On top of all this, here is The Telegraph sending the

money for this column to Tom Loyless—and so far I don't even get postage back.

Nevertheless, there is one redeeming feature about Georgia newspapers—they are more or less Democratic in their editorial tone. That is one reason why my digestion is perfect down here. Back home my digestion starts the day all right, but after reading the morning papers at the breakfast table, things go wrong. By the time I have finished reading the evening papers, I am a hopeless dyspeptic.

Honestly, though, you people in Georgia have no conception of the odds under which Northern Democrats labor. Take, for instance, upstate New York—i.e., all the State outside of New York City. Over 90 per cent of the daily papers and over 90 per cent of the local weekly papers are Republican through and through. It isn't even an intelligent Republicanism. Politically they form one vast combine. There is practically no individual editorship, practically no independent comment or thought. They are organized almost 100 per cent to keep harping on and disseminating the carefully prepared propaganda of the Republican organization.

Let me give you an example. Last February there was published in New York State an analysis by me of figures showing that the Democratic vote in New York State as a whole was definitely an increasing vote in proportion to that for Republican candidates. My figures went back for five years, covered all candidates from President down, and were taken from the official returns. The conclusion was so favorable to the Democratic party, especially in those localities where active organization work had been carried on, that the Republican organization realized that they had been hard hit.

What happened? Within a month, over sixty upstate newspapers had commented on the figures and in the same language, word for word, from beginning to end. In other words, the Republican State committee bureau had written out an editorial form of answer, which deliberately garbled my official figures, and tried to reply to fact by ridicule. And this made-to-order widely disseminated stuff was grabbed and used by the Republican press (i.e., by practically the whole press in upstate New York).

It seems to me, that for the good of the average man and woman in this country, it is better to have papers carry the individual opinions of their owners and editors—as they do in Georgia—than to be the mere hirelings of a well-oiled political organization, as they are in the North. This is based, of course, on the assumption that down here the average reader reads more than one paper. In upstate New York, even if you do read several papers, you get precisely the same opinions from each, and generally in the same language. Down here, it is a liberal education to read, for example, the editorial comments of The Macon Telegraph, the Atlanta Constitution and the Atlanta Journal, the same day.

However, I must not get mixed up in Georgia politics. You people can mix it up to your hearts' content over all the local matters in the world just so long as you come together and work shoulder to shoulder when it comes to national issues and the general strengthening and better organization of the Democratic party throughout the United States.

I shall send this off before T. W. L. comes back with the wild flowers—otherwise he might edit it.

Warm Springs, Ga.   FRANKLIN D. ROOSEVELT

2

"The Matter of Woods and Trees and Lumber in General"

Saturday, April 18, 1925

THINGS ARE running more smoothly now—T.W.L. is
still picking wild flowers and sticking them in pots 'round
the "OLD SWIMMIN' HOLE," and in a few days more will
forget that he was ever in the newspaper game. That leaves
me free to exploit some of my own particular hobbies.

What I want to boil over about today is the matter of
woods and trees and lumber in general. Yesterday afternoon
I went up to the top of Pine Mountain. There, stretching
out for many miles to the horizon, was a large portion of
Merriwether County. It was good looking country—and
good to live in. In many ways it reminded me of the views
I get from hilltops in my own Dutchess County, back from
the Hudson River, and I might add that the people who live
in it are very much the same type of American citizen as they
are back home where I came from.

31

But there in front of me, in the middle distance, two thick columns of smoke were rising in the quiet air. "Burning off the woods," somebody said.

The same thing is happening by accident or design in every State in the Union. I have not got the definite statistics with me, but in this country of ours we burn up, through ground or forest fires, somewhere between $200,000,000 or $300,000,000 worth of standing timber every year.

Who pays? Why, you do—every reader of this paper, and of every other paper. An adequate timber supply is wealth to a nation. To burn it up before it is used is precisely the same as burning down a house, or throwing dollar bills into the fire.

It costs twice as much to build a wooden house today as it did ten years ago, and the increase is not by any means due solely to the higher cost of labor. Everybody who reads knows, of course, that we, the American people, are using each year twice as much lumber as the natural growth of trees matures.

Up to a short time ago, for instance, the State of Georgia exported millions of feet of lumber to other States in the North. One of your State officials told me last week that he doubted if this State today cuts enough lumber for the needs of its own citizens. You export some, of course, through Jacksonville and Brunswick and Savannah, but on the other hand, you import a goodly amount by rail.

The real question is this: What are you doing with the acres from which timber has been taken? Is the second growth being treated as a crop—guarded against hogs and cattle and fire, so that in 25 to 30 years you will again be able to harvest the crop? No one objects, of course, if cut-over land is turned by the plow and put to raising of peaches or cotton

32

or other productive crops. But a vast amount—the majority—of your cut-over lands are not suitable for agriculture. They are suitable, however, for a crop of trees, as is proved by the millions of dollars' worth of lumber already taken off them.

The man in the city takes but little interest in this question; nor, I am sorry to say, does the man on the farm, though it is of vital concern to both of them. I don't know what laws you have in the State of Georgia on this subject—very few, and very inadequate they must be as my personal observation in this section and in other parts of the State testifies. We, in this country, still have a tremendous amount to learn from older civilizations. Many of the nations of Europe found themselves, about 150 years ago, practically stripped of their forest. They learned that individuals are, as individuals, essentially selfish—that if it was left to the sweet will of the individual land owner he would not bother his head to plant new trees or protect young seedlings where he had cut off his original piece of timber. Over in Europe the timber shortage became so acute that the governments had to step in and create State forests.

Like most Democrats, I am pretty thoroughly opposed to having the Federal, or even the State governments, embark in new enterprises which should be handled by individuals, but unless we, in the United States, take immediate steps to compel the growing of new timber by individuals, I prophesy that it will become a government enterprise in the next generation. The national supply is decreasing so fast that we already import vast quantities, but even the world's supply of virgin forest is exhaustible.

I suppose some of my Republican friends would call me a

Socialist for asserting that the owner of land owes it to the community, and to the State, and to the nation, to use that land in the best possible way for humanity. It is fine talk and very soothing to think of the individual as complete master in his own home, at perfect liberty to do any old thing he wants with his own property. A man has the legal right to go to his bank, draw out his balance in paper money, go home and put it in the stove. If he does it, however, he is apt to land in the lunatic asylum. We have not yet reached the common-sense age which will, in like manner, send the farmer who burns off his wood lot to the home for incurables!

It comes, in the final analysis, to this: The day will arrive when, by law or custom or some other way, the farmer with, say, 100 acres of land, 20 of which are not of the right sort for raising agricultural crops, will use those 20 acres to grow a crop of commercially valuable trees.

It is exceedingly hard to persuade a man to plant or care for a crop which will not mature until possibly he, himself, is dead and gone. That was the trouble in Europe in the olden days. I suppose that when the first white settlers came into this part of Georgia, about 100 years ago, they found so much magnificent virgin forest, that they exclaimed, "It is an inexhaustible supply." Their great grandchildren have been kicking for a good many years now because there is none of it left.

In spite of all this we do give a good deal of thought to the well-being of our descendants. More and more we build for the future. In 1850 few could visualize a nation of 110,000,000 people 75 years later. It is hard for us to think of a United States of 200,000,000 people in 1975. When that day comes Georgia, for instance, will probably have twice its present population—50 years from now! It will be an increase not confined to the cities—it will be an increase due not just to the birthrate in existing Georgia families. Last Fall the Governor of this State made a speech on the subject of "Georgia for the Georgians." I, myself, know enough people in Georgia to know that he did not speak for the State. If every State adopted that attitude we should have, in a generation, an aggregation of 48 ingrowing, inbred selfish communities. Incidentally the rest of the country won't let Georgia keep itself for Georgians. Fortunately, or unfortunately, for yourselves, your State is much too attractive. People from other places want to come here, and if you keep up the delightful hospitality of your individual citizens, you will have thousands and thousands of new faces in your midst in the days to come.

FRANKLIN D. ROOSEVELT

Warm Springs, Ga.

3

"We Lack a Sense of Humor If We Forget That Not So Very Long Ago We Were Immigrants Ourselves"

Tuesday, April 21, 1925

THIS COLUMN job seems to be still mine. T.W.L. had to quit picking wild flowers and building what he calls roads on Pine Mountain, and devote himself to the people who have insisted on coming to Warm Springs before the season is opened. He ought to have lived in Georgia long enough to know that for some people it is "open season" all the year around. Just now, he is putting up beds and borrowing cottages and establishing a commissary department, and my only fear is that he will insist on going back to this column-writing as a recreation. You know he writes in his sleep!

Coincidences are funny things. Also, this United States is a mighty small place. Yesterday I read two "letters to the editor." One from a farmer in Georgia to an Atlanta paper; the other from a farmer in New York to an upstate paper. Both letters were aimed against any proposal to increase

European immigration to the country, and both referred to Europeans in general as "ignorant peasants, whose living conditions are those of beasts."

Now, I don't want to take up in any way the actual numbers of immigrants we should let in each year. But I do want to suggest that a person who classes all farmers in every European country as "ignorant," or as living under bestial conditions, is just plain common or garden "ignorant" himself, and the odds are 100 to 1 that his own living conditions are not up to what we would like to call the American standard.

Generalizations of this sort by Americans are even sillier than the generalizations of European writers who spend three weeks in the United States, go back home and write two volumes on "America As I Found It."

It goes without saying that no sensible American wants this country to be made a dumping ground for foreigners of any nation, but it is equally true that there are a great many foreigners who, if they came here, would make exceedingly desirable citizens. It becomes, therefore, in the first place, a question of selection. We can take a leaf out of the note-book of our Canadian friends in regard to this. The Canadian Government has well-equipped agents in the different European countries. If an individual or a family wishes to emigrate to Canada application is made to this agent, who, thereupon, carefully inspects the individual or the family, passes upon their mental ability, moral soundness, conditions of health and general desirability. This seems a more reasonable and practical method than waiting until the emigrant reaches the immigration station at Ellis Island in New York Harbor.

In one other respect our Canadian neighbors have a far

better system than ours. Their policy is to prevent large groups of foreign born from congregating in any one locality. In other words, they seek distribution of their immigrants throughout every portion of Canada. When the individual or family in the European country applies to the Canadian agent for permission to come over he must agree to go to one of the sections of Canada which is not already too full of foreigners. If, twenty-five years ago, the United States had adopted a policy of this kind we would not have the huge foreign sections which exist in so many of our cities.

Experience in every State of the Union shows that a little new European blood of the right sort does a lot of good in any community. Let me give you an example. A certain agricultural county in a Northern State which I am very familiar with prided itself, up to perhaps twenty-five years ago, that its inhabitants came almost wholly from the old English and Scotch stock with a small admixture of the first Dutch settlers' blood. That county was rich in false pride and in mighty little else. Its agriculture was of no higher quality than it had been in the year 1800. Its schools barely complied with the minimum of the law—its internal improvements were about as they had been three generations ago.

Into that community there came, by chance I think, about a dozen families from Southern Germany. They were called peasants and looked down on as such. But their education was better than that of the old families among whom they settled, their morals were higher and their willingness and desire to improve conditions in general was more truly American than that of their neighbors. Within ten years each one of these new families had made good. Their farms were better kept, their living conditions on a higher standard than those of their neighbors—and they were making more money. Today these families are a part of the community, thoroughly Americanized, intermarried with the old stock and every one admits that the increasing prosperity and progressiveness of that county is due largely to their example. A few years later some other families came in from Northern Italy, the right type of emigrant—they, too, have borne and are bearing their share in the general improvement of conditions.

Taking it by and large, I agree that for a good many years to come European immigration should remain greatly restricted. We have, unfortunately, a great many thousand foreigners who got in here and who must be digested. For fifty years the United States ate a meal altogether too large—much of the food was digestible, but some of it was almost poisonous. The United States must, for a short time at least, stop eating, and when it resumes should confine itself to the most readily assimilable foodstuffs. In the meantime we can all help in this digestive process by encouraging these foreigners to break away from their own little foreign groups in our large cities. Many of them, in our cities, come of good, sound stock and would make thoroughly acceptable neighbors in the farming communities. We would be helping not only them, but ourselves, also.

Incidentally, we lack a sense of humor and of proportion if we forget that not so very long ago we were immigrants ourselves. Scarcely a family which comes of so-called old American stock, but has the blood of various nationalities in its veins. It is only a question of going back a few generations, more or less.

Don't forget that some of the most backward and ignorant sections of the United States in the Northern and Southern States are sections populated almost exclusively with the so-called "pure American stock." On this very great question involving our future, no one has a right to speak without a pretty good first-hand knowledge of the whole of the United States.

Once upon a time, when a certain relation of mine was President, he had been blocked on some national measures because too many Congressmen were unable to see beyond the confines of their own districts. The President was heard to remark: "I wish I could be President and Congress too for just five minutes: I would pass a law requiring every candidate for Congress to file an affidavit that he had visited every State in the Union." There is a good deal in the thought.

FRANKLIN D. ROOSEVELT

Warm Springs, Ga.

4

"A Little Matter Involving the Expenditure of About $3,000,000,000 Each Year"

Thursday, April 23, 1925

IN MY VISITS to Georgia I have met so many citizens who have such a sense of civic duty and desire for progress, that I was venturing to talk out loud on a subject to which I have given more than passing attention and which I have seen at very close range for a good many years. I am referring to the efficiency of the administration of our national government—a little matter involving the expenditure of about $3,000,000,000 each year and affecting the lives and pocketbooks of every man, woman and child in the United States. It may take two or three issues of this paper to cover even the high spots, but I hope that what I say may provoke discussion and interest even if you do not all agree with me.

First of all, a few words on history. After the formation of the first government under the Constitution, in 1789, President George Washington was confronted with a task almost as difficult as that of organizing the Revolutionary Army—but a task of an entirely different character. The Constitution did not provide for the machinery of government; it left that to laws enacted by Congress. Even that first Congress was jealous of the President and in creating the original departments it provided not a lump sum appropriation for each department, but enacted into law the details of how many employes there should be, what their duties should be, and how much pay they should receive. The nation was deeply in debt, the revenue was problematical and even at the outset the scale of pay for the Federal employes was made a good deal lower than pay for similar work in private life.

As a result President Washington had real difficulty not only in finding cabinet officers who could afford to give up their business to serve their country, but difficulty also in filling the subordinate positions with men who were qualified for their tasks. In addition to this he faced an enormous demand for soft jobs from Revolutionary soldiers who honestly believed that their services in the war entitled them to clerkships and other Federal employment even if they could neither read nor write. The result was that the Federal service started off on a relatively inefficient basis.

The next step was the rise of political parties, and the political bitterness which started about the time of John Quincy Adams and Andrew Jackson gave rise to the perfectly human doctrine "To the Victors Belong the Spoils," because no administration wanted to be surrounded by subordinates who might at any time work politically against their chiefs.

Things went from bad to worse, and the depths of inefficiency and political plunder were reached in the '70's during the administration of President Grant. The giving of political favors was naturally followed by the granting of private favors, and corruption in those days reached even into the Cabinet of the President himself—I might draw a comparison, but I won't.

This was the real origin of the nation-wide demand for an efficient and non-partisan Civil Service Reform. President Cleveland was its great disciple. It was based on the obvious promise that the thousands of government employes should be chosen for their fitness to do the work rather than for their political affiliations and influence. From that day to this the overwhelming majority of the Federal employes (with the exception of postmasters) have been chosen through the competitive examinations administered by the Civil Service Commission.

No reasonable person who has studied the workings of the Federal Government can deny that the result has been a vast improvement over the former spoils system, and Civil Service methods have been rapidly extended to practically all State and municipal employes. The nation as a whole was so well satisfied that a great reform had been put through that for forty years it has assumed that the result had brought efficiency and honesty, in place of incapacity and corruption.

Civil Service did end corruption. That I can say as a broad statement applying to the overwhelming majority of Federal employes. They are as a class honest and faithful in the services they give to the government which employs them.

But the question of the efficiency of the government is a very different story, and one which is not a reflection on the employes themselves, but rather on the antiquated system of

43

promotion and pay. Everything is comparative, and when I make the above statement I am comparing in my mind the government system with the systems of employment used by successful private employers—those who have made good with large businesses and who at the same time are thoroughly progressive in giving the best of treatment and consideration to their employes. It is not going too far to assert that no successful private business could keep out of bankruptcy for six months if it substituted government employment system for its own.

The key to the whole problem lies in this: A successful private employer, as the government does, satisfies himself as to the character and capacity of each employe when that employe is first taken in at the bottom of the ladder. There the similarity ceases. The private employer makes careful note of the ability and capacity of the individual also after the work has commenced—he promotes the more efficient and discharges the inefficient. This system holds good all the way up the ladder. The most capable employes rise rapidly. Those less efficient rise more slowly, and the inefficient are discharged.

With government employment the basis is wholly different —it is altogether too much predicated on seniority. In other words, after the Civil Service Commission has passed on the original application, and the employe has been sworn in, he or she is practically certain of a life job whether efficient or not. Discharge from the government service on the ground of lack of capacity is a very rare thing. It would not be so bad if promotion from one grade to another were based on competition. As things stand now this promotion is based altogether too much on longevity of service. It is true that the government employes have to pass some sort of nominal examination when they go from one grade to another. But the promotion itself comes primarily as a result of long service and at the instigation of the Bureau Chief or Chief Clerk of the department.

The remedy for this state of affairs is to make promotion competitive and to place it in the hands of somebody such as the Civil Service Commission which will keep it out of politics, thereby rewarding those who deserve it, eliminating the deadwood and making our government service worthy of the nation.

That, however, is only half the way of accomplishing the purpose, as I shall point out if T. W. Loyless and the editor of this delightful paper allow me to write this column again.

FRANKLIN D. ROOSEVELT

Warm Springs, Ga.

5

"I Am About to Continue My Delicate Suggestions That the Federal Civil Service Needs a Doctor"

Sunday, April 26, 1925

AS NOBODY has yet sought to get out an injunction against me for writing this column, I am about to continue my delicate suggestions that the Federal Civil Service needs a doctor.

I pointed out the other day that practically all the government departments need a brand-new system of promotion. Something must be done to allow the most capable employes to rise and to allow the least capable employes to return gracefully to private life.

Something like this would do worlds of good—but the mere fact of the creation of a promotion system recognizing merit will not in itself and all alone give us an efficient government. Every year thousands of young men and young women enter the employ of Uncle Sam. They do so for many different kinds of reasons, some because there is a certain honor and credit attached to this form of public service, others because they feel it will give them experience in their chosen field of work. As things are now, however, it is the rule rather than the exception that the most capable and efficient of these young men and women sooner or later leave the government and obtain positions with private employers.

I have pointed out that the lack of an adequate promotion system is one reason why the departments lose so many of their most valued workers.

The other reason is the very human one of dollars and cents. Government employment should be and will be some day a real career. Today it is not. Private business of all kinds offers so many greater inducements that it is only natural that the best government employes so often leave.

The whole scale of government pay is on a false basis. I am not referring, of course, to the higher officials of the administration, such as the appointed members of the cabinet. It is true that most men who go into the average cabinet are capable of making more on the outside than the $15,000 a year which the law now allows. It is also true that it costs most of them more to live in Washington in official life than it would back home in private life. Furthermore, we have well-known examples of cabinet members such as Secretary McAdoo and Secretary Lane who simply had to resign or go heavily into debt.

The people I am referring to are the non-political employes who come under the civil service laws. Let me give you some examples: If you enter a government department as a young man as a clerk on, say, a salary of $1,100 a year, and rise through all the grades to that of Chief Clerk of the Department, in the course of the next thirty years, you will be getting, perhaps, the princely salary of $3,800 or $4,000 a year. As Chief Clerk you are what might be called the General Manager of the business—only the cabinet officer and his assistant are over you; you are the permanent head, while they come and go with succeeding administrations. As Chief Clerk or General Manager, you have the supervision of thousands of employes under you. You have to see that the shop is running smoothly and efficiently, that the output is satisfactory and that the overhead is low. If you were in a similar position with some private business, it would be a business operating all over the United States with all sorts of branches and you would be getting a salary of somewhere between $20,000 and $50,000 a year. Yet your parsimonious Uncle Sam asks you to do the same character of work for $4,000 a year or less.

Take the Civil Service employes of the next grade. Each department of the Federal Government is divided into Bureaus. Many of these bureaus employ thousands of people each, and over them is a bureau chief clerk. He, too, is at the top of the ladder. He has gone as far as he possibly can go in his government career with the exception of the chief clerkship of the whole department. He gets the magnificent salary of $2,400 or $2,600 a year. If he were working in a similar capacity for a private concern, i.e., as the head of a branch office, or subdivision, he would get a salary of from $10,000 to $20,000 a year. It is a good deal of strain on the imagination for the poor fellow in Washington to keep on working for a quarter or an eighth of the sum.

Is the government doing a fair thing? It seems to me that

a great nation like the United States should pay adequate salaries. As a broad principle there is no reason why the United States should not pay approximately the salaries which are paid on the average by private employers. That does not mean that the government should pay a member of the cabinet $100,000 a year just because some private corporation is silly enough to pay him that in private life, but it does mean that the government employes should be able to look forward to just and reasonable compensation if they make good and reach the top of the ladder.

For instance, if the chief clerk of a government department has under him 5,000 employes, a salary of $10,000 a year would not seem exactly extravagant. A private corporation would pay a good deal more to a manager in a similar position. So, too, the chief clerk of a bureau could receive $5,000 or $6,000 a year and still be underpaid in comparison with private concerns.

I shudder to think what would happen if the government of the United States were to reorganize the salaries of its departmental employes from the top down. A new career and a real career would be opened to American boys and girls. They would no longer treat government service as a mere stepping stone to something better. They would strive to make good within the service itself. They would know that if they did make good they could reach the top and with the attainment of the goal be assured of enough income to support their families in the right way, to lay up something for a rainy day, and to make their own departments models of efficiency. There would be a new note of pride which, I am sorry to say, is today woefully lacking.

There would be a new note of pride, too, in the American people themselves. It has been and is, our practice, to expect efficiency from government. Unfortunately this shameful attitude comes too much from experience. Would it not be one of the most magnificent and progressive feats of the Republic if within the next generation we could turn completely around and point to the government of the United States as the model for all the employers of the country? Would it not give us a wonderful feeling if we knew that our government, for efficiency of service and for fairness to its workers, was the best government in the world instead of one of the worst?

FRANKLIN D. ROOSEVELT

Warm Springs, Ga.

6

"The Next Great Contribution to the American Republic Will Be the Placing of Its Administrative Affairs on a Business Basis"

Tuesday, April 28, 1925

I CAN ALMOST hear some of the readers of this paper saying "This Roosevelt fellow wants to raise the government salaries; isn't the cost of government high enough already?" That is where I am going to fool you. I am perfectly willing to go on record and say that you could raise the pay of the men and women in the higher, more responsible Civil Service government positions 50 per cent or even 100 per cent, and still have the government cost no more.

This I say with the sole reservation that we must establish with the increase in salaries a system of promotion based on merit and capacity only. Human nature makes people more efficient where they are guaranteed promotion and better pay. It is, after all, the average which counts. If the AVERAGE young man or young woman entering a government department in the lowest grade were convinced that slack work would mean a polite discharge and excellent work a deserved promotion, and if, further, they knew that if they eventually rose to or near the top, they would receive a salary commensurate with their ability, their output of work would in many cases be doubled. Initiative would take the place of routine—ambition would take the place of easy-going slackness.

I know one young man who went into a Washington department as a typist; he was a fast and accurate worker. The first day he was there he was given a lot of one page letters similar in character, to typewrite. At 4:30 that afternoon he took 45 completed letters to the chief clerk of his bureau. When he got back to his desk the typist next to him asked him how many he had turned out, and on his replying "45" the typist gathered several other workers who gently but firmly led my friend aside and told him that he would have to change his output immediately. The customary output per typist per day was only 24 letters, and he was informed that unless he limited himself to 24 letters he would get into trouble.

I do not make the accusation that this sort of thing is general through the government service, but it is true that there is very little incentive for the turning out of the best and most rapid kind of work. On the whole you cannot blame these men and women because they know that extra ability will not advance them more quickly than if they do just enough to get by with it, and they are constantly reminded of the fact that even if they do rise to near the top they will be getting hardly any increase of pay.

A merit promotion system, with adequate salaries to look

forward to, would enable the average of our 10 government departments, and our 20 to 30 commissions and bureaus, not connected with any department, to cut their working forces from 10 to 15 per cent. Assume, for example, one government department with a total annual payroll of $10,000,000. I am perfectly certain that a proper system of promotion and of getting rid of the deadwood would save at least $1,000,000 of this, and the other 90 per cent of the employes who are left would be fully capable of doing, and doing better, the work of the original 100 per cent. If, then, the government were to take half of the $1,000,000 thus saved and add it to the pay, in the high grades, there would still be a net saving to the taxpayers of $500,000 each year.

Ever since the beginning of our government Congress has thought it necessary to legislate for the number of workers to be employed in every government office. That would not be so bad, but Congress goes further and legislates the exact number to be employed in each grade and the exact pay for every individual so employed. I have never heard of the President or the directors of a large and successful private business wasting their time going over the employment and salary roll of each and every one of their departments. What they do is this: in consultation with their employment managers they establish a general scale of salaries—so much for the managers, so much for the assistants, so much for the clerks, so much for the experts, and so on all the way down the line. Once this is done, they turn the schedule over to the department head; they say to him: "This is the scale of salaries to be paid —this is the system of promotion to be used; go to it; run your department as economically and as efficiently as you can

—you are responsible to us for results." If the department head fails to make good, he is fired and they get a new one.

Some day, perhaps the Congress of the United States will give the heads of the great government departments more latitude. Congress should, of course, establish by law the general scale of salaries and a uniform system of promotions. After that Congress should tell the department heads to go to it and make good. It is a perfectly simple thing for our Congress, and with far less waste of energy than at present, to keep a check on the success of the department heads in just the same way as the president and directors of a private business would.

During the past few years we have been operating our national government under the so-called budget system. This is, without doubt, a great step—but only one step in advance. The budget system was first recommended by President Wilson, largely as a result of the experience gained during the World War. A Republican Congress denied the budget system to President Wilson, but granted it in substantially the same form to President Harding the following year. Much boasting has been done in regard to the budget system. Partisans have claimed that at least the government is on a business basis. As a matter of fact, while the budget system has done undoubted good in the matter of estimating government expenses for the ensuing year, and has helped Congress and the Treasury and the people of the United States in knowing the totals of their income and of their expenditure it has failed utterly to establish efficiency in the actual spending of the money.

Many people, in and out of public life, have, during the past ten years or more, discussed a complete reorganization of the government departments, and of government employment as a whole. Commissions have been appointed, and have taken volumes of testimony. Nothing has happened.

The next great contribution which will be made to the cause of the American Republic will be the placing of its administrative affairs on a business basis. Then, at last, will government service become a career worthy of the ambition and effort of every young American starting out on life's work.

FRANKLIN D. ROOSEVELT

Warm Springs, Ga.

7

"The Average American and the Average Japanese Have Very Cloudy and Often Erroneous Points of View About Relations Between the Two Countries"

Thursday, April 30, 1925

WE HAVE BEEN reading during the past few days about the "attack" on Hawaii by part of the American Navy and the "defense" of the islands by another part and by the Army and local Militia. A few months ago the flamboyant public announcement of these maneuvers by the Administration in Washington caused a distinct flurry of public feeling and adverse criticism in Japan, and certainly did little to enhance the cause of peace between Japan and the United States. It was the manner of the announcement, rather than the actual holding of maneuvers by the Navy off our Pacific seaboard. Japan could have raised no possible argument if the maneuvers had been announced for what they were—the working out of the problem of the defense of the Pacific Coast in precisely the same broad manner as we have worked out problems on several occasions relating to the defense of the Atlantic Coast and adjoining waters. For Hawaii bears a somewhat similar relation to the Pacific seaboard that Guantanamo and Porto Rico and the Virgin Islands do to the Atlantic seaboard.

In this connection the average American and the average Japanese have very cloudy and often erroneous points of view about the relations between the two countries. What could be more simple than for jingoes and trouble makers and pessimists to point out that Japan is the dominant power in wealth and in military resources on the Western side of the Pacific, that the United States occupies the same position on the Eastern side, and that a clash of interest is inevitable. These dangerous agitators then point out the bogey of Japanese immigration and the Japanese infiltration into what they call our privileged commercial markets. Japanese jingoes, at the same time, complain of American insults through exclusion laws and the pretensions of America to the control of the trade of China and other parts of the Far East.

Let us first examine that nightmare to many Americans, especially our friends in California, the growing population of Japanese on the Pacific slope. It is undoubtedly true that in the past many thousands of Japanese have legally or otherwise got into the United States, settled here and raised children who become American citizens. Californians have properly objected on the sound basic ground that Japanese immigrants are not capable of assimilation into the American population.

If this had throughout the discussion been made the sole ground for the American attitude all would have been well, and the people of Japan would today understand and accept our decision.

Anyone who has traveled in the Far East knows that the mingling of Asiatic blood with European or American blood produces, in nine cases out of ten, the most unfortunate results. There are, throughout the East, many thousands of so-called Eurasians—men and women and children partly of Asiatic blood and partly of European or American blood. These Eurasians are, as a common thing, looked down on and despised, both by the European and American who resides there, and by the pure Asiatic who lives there.

The argument works both ways. I know a great many cultivated, highly educated and delightful Japanese. They have all told me that they would feel the same repugnance and objection to have thousands of Americans settle in Japan and intermarry with the Japanese as I would feel in having large numbers of Japanese come over here and intermarry with the American population.

In this question, then, of Japanese exclusion from the United States, it is necessary only to advance the true reason— the undesirability of mixing the blood of the two peoples. This attitude would be fully understood in Japan, as they would have the same objection to Americans migrating to Japan in large numbers.

Unfortunately, Japanese exclusion has been urged for many other reasons—their ability to work for and live on much smaller wages than Americans—their willingness to work for longer hours; their driving out of native Americans from certain fruit-growing or agricultural areas. The Japanese themselves do not understand these arguments and are offended by them.

As to commercial rivalry, as the cause for a clash between the two nations, I fail utterly to see that the argument has weight. Our principal commercial rival throughout the years has been Great Britain and yet this has not been advanced as a reason for a pending war with her. The civilization of Japan is far older than our own, and in the field of the philosophy of life the Japanese regard us as children who are passing through the stage which they, themselves, underwent 1,000 years ago. Yet it was not until a generation ago that the Japanese nation decided to emulate the Western nations in material things. Since that time, Japan has made almost unbelievable strides. She manufactures today almost every known article, and is competing with American and European nations in selling these articles all over the world. It is true that the cost of manufacture in Japan is, on the whole, far below what it is here, but it is true also that the cost of manufacture in many European countries is also far lower than in the United States. As Japan advances in successful materialism her wage scale, her conditions of living and her cost of production, therefore, will increase until the difference is no longer so great.

In other words, economic conditions tend to seek the same level. We are, today, competitors with Japan in many of the markets of the world. Is that a cause for war? Often I have thought that those materialists who assert that all wars are caused by economic and trade rivalries ought to be put in the insane asylum. History shows us many wars in which trade rivalry had but little part. History shows us, on the other hand, countless wars which were brought about by prejudice, by a misstatement of facts—by religious fanaticism—by hastily spoken words.

The Japanese people and the American people are both opposed to intermarriage of the two races—there can be no quarrel there. The Japanese people and the American people do not want to invade each other's countries—there can be no quarrel there. The Japanese people and the American people both seek trade expansion in legitimate channels and under fair conditions of world wide competition—that is not a cause for war. The Japanese Navy is at perfect liberty to carry out so-called strategic problems involving the defense of their coast. We have the same right with respect to our own coasts. But it is hardly tactful for the American Government to give its own citizens, and the Japanese nation as well, the impression in seeking publicity for the Navy that we are trying to find out how easy or how difficult it would be for the Japanese Navy to occupy Hawaii preparatory to a descent on our own Pacific coast!

FRANKLIN D. ROOSEVELT

Warm Springs, Ga.

8

"Every American Wants to See This Country Lead in the Advancement of Civilization, And in the Lessening, Not Only of the Horrors of War, But of the Chances of War Itself"

Saturday, May 2, 1925

S PEAKING of the Navy, I am reminded of a trip which I made to Georgia and Mississippi soon after I went to the Navy Department in 1913. The good people of Brunswick, Ga., and of Biloxi, Miss., were anxious to have the Federal Government establish naval stations in their harbors. The harbor entrance in both cases proved too shallow, but I had delightful visits in both cities. Brunswick I remember chiefly for the possum banquet they gave me—every known variety of possum cooked in every known variety of style. I ate them all.

At Biloxi I was deeply interested in having Congressman Pat Harrison, now Senator, drive me over to visit Jefferson Davis' splendid home.

It was on this trip, however, that I first formed the idea of the need in modern naval warfare for a complete chain of anti-submarine and anti-aircraft stations the whole length of our coast. It was obvious that in time of peace the Navy Department could not possibly have enough money each year to maintain such stations, yet it was obvious to me we should need them in time of war. Even in 1913, submarines had attained ocean-going size, and aircraft flown from the decks of battleships were being experimented with. The principle [sic] harbors of the United States were, of course, guarded, but a successful patrol of the whole coast required, I thought, patrol bases at least not more than 100 miles apart.

When I got back to Washington I tried to get the General Board of the Navy Department to prepare a plan of coast patrol for use in the event of war, but the General Board did not think it worth while to bother its head about such little matters. It is amusing to note that a couple of months before we actually got into the World War, in 1917, the higher naval officers did a lot of running around and planning for the Naval patrol stations which we maintained throughout the war.

Have people forgotten already the tremendous sensation caused by the German submarines after 1914? Here again is a slice of history. When the European War broke out, in 1914, news came through from German sources that they expected the submarines to be a serious menace to the British control of the seas. In the Navy Department in Washington it was the general rule among the older officers to minimize the potentialities of the submarine, and to discredit any thought of their exercising a very large effect on allied commerce or supplies. Many of the younger officers, however, saw in the German submarines a real threat and with them I agreed. We believed, nevertheless, that if the German submarines were temporarily successful in destroying a large allied tonnage some answer to the submarine would eventually be found. This also proved to be correct, and by the Autumn of 1918 submarines had been in a broad sense placed under control.

This is but a proof of the old, historical fact that every new offensive weapon meets, in time, a defensive weapon which neutralizes its power. Back at the beginning of the War between the States, enthusiasts believed that the new high powered rifled guns would end naval warfare because no wooden ship could withstand them. We know, however, that almost simultaneously the use of armor plate on ships neutralized the added power of the new guns. So with submarines. They have become one of the many weapons of offensive warfare, and various forms of defense are now used against them.

Another controversy is now raising—whether the airplane has, or has not, put the older weapons wholly out of existence. Judging by history, it has not. For instance, the torpedo boat of 40 years ago was going to render all battleships obsolete. Ten years ago the submarine was going to do the same thing. Today the prophecy is made for the airplane, but the probability is that aircraft will merely take their place as additional weapons of warfare, and not as new weapons which supersede and drive out of existence all the old ones.

This, however, brings up the most serious phase of future wars. Airplanes can reach portions of an enemy's country hitherto safely "behind the lines." In the recent war many hundreds of people were killed and wounded—men, women and children—by airplane bombs far back of the lines in France, Germany and England. Since the war ended great discoveries have been made in the use of fatal gases, it being claimed that whole city populations could be destroyed by a single enemy plane.

If that be true, the world faces a problem far greater than the mere limitation of armaments.

Largely as a result of the writings of the great Dutchman Grotius, 300 years ago, the treatment of enemy civilian populations in time of war became more humane and more civilized throughout Europe. With few exceptions the so-called "rules of war" then laid down were maintained fairly well until the World War. Then, largely because of the German doctrine of terrorism, civilian populations were treated as combatants would be. If in the next war nations feel themselves at liberty to destroy and injure the enemy civilian populations outside of the actual fighting zone, we shall go back to the unlimited and horrible conditions of warfare in the Dark and Middle Ages.

It would seem to be more important that this tremendous subject be discussed fully and frankly by the civilized nations now, in time of peace, than that there should be a mere international conference to plan for the scrapping of a few more battleships.

What is the United States going to do about it? Our position as a leader in such a great cause is clearer than that of any other nation. We are separated by thousands of miles of ocean from any other power formidable as a military antagonist. We seek no aggrandizement of territory. The world as a whole will follow our lead more readily than that of any other nation. Yet the present government in Washington mouths around about "entangling alliances" and a "hands off" policy. No American, of course, wants any entangling alliance, but every American wants to see this country play the part of a man and lead in the advancement of civilization as a whole, and in the lessening, not only of the horrors of war, but of the chances of war itself. Are you satisfied, by the way, that America is today doing its full duty to mankind?

FRANKLIN D. ROOSEVELT

Warm Springs, Ga.

9

"A Hodgepodge of Direct and Indirect Taxes"

Tuesday, May 5, 1925

TODAY I have a letter from one of your readers in Marshallville, suggesting I take up the subject of "Taxation in Georgia." I suppose that, since I have become a newspaper man, this ought to be easy, especially in view of the fact that I never set up to be a tax expert or to know anything about Georgia taxes.

However, here go some random thoughts on a problem which at least ought to interest every citizen. Historically the United States derives its methods of government and law far more from England than from continental Europe, and it would be supposed that our system of taxation in America would follow more closely the English methods rather than the continental. Yet, this is not the case. In England, and in most of her colonies, direct taxes on property have, as a general proposition, yielded the bulk of the revenue, whereas in continental Europe indirect taxes have been the rule.

Here in the Unitd States, we have a hodgepodge of direct

and indirect taxes, and have inclined more to the indirect form than to the English method. The different individual States, without regard to sectional lines, present all sorts of systems; in other words, we have no uniform theory, and there is much confusion and resulting inequalities and injustices. Similarly, no line is drawn between Federal taxes and State taxes. Often there is double taxation because of a lack of a system.

Let me give some examples: In New York State, the individual has to pay a double income tax—one to Washington, the other to Albany—and when the individual dies his estate has to pay a double inheritance tax—one Federal and one State. In Georgia, the individual has to pay, I think, only the Federal income tax, but his estate has to pay a double inheritance tax. In New York, cigars and cigarettes have to pay only the Federal tax. In Georgia, they have to pay, in addition, a State tax.

The day will undoubtedly come when, by legislation or by common consent, a clearly drawn line of demarkation will be fixed between the individual States, on the one hand, and the Federal Government on the other, and sooner that day comes, the better. If certain classes of taxes were reserved for the Federal Government, and other classes for the State government, double taxes would be avoided and the whole system, both local and national, would be put on a basis which the average tax payer could understand. This would result in more thought being given by our legislators, with resulting increase in responsibility of government—a thing to be greatly desired.

I understand that the bulk of your taxes in Georgia are

direct and in two forms: First, the direct tax on land and realty, and secondly, the direct tax on personal property. I am told also that the direct tax on land is unequally administered in the different counties of the State. For instance, one county may assess at 50 per cent of the full value of the land and another county at 60 to 70 per cent. So, also, the tax rate in one county may be only half as great as the tax rate in another county. A man with a farm actually worth $10,000 in one section of the State may pay taxes twice as great as a man who owns a farm of exactly the same value in another section.

Georgia is not by any means the only State which suffers from these inequalities. In general, State laws provide, or intend to provide, for uniform taxation, but the way these laws are carried out absolutely nullifies the purpose. In the State of New York, [where] county valuation and county rates vary also, a distinct effort has been made, during the past few years, by the State Board of Equalization to bring about a more uniform assessment and tax rate.

Many States are wholly abandoning the direct tax on personal property as distinguished from real estate. For instance, in New York State, the personal tax on household furniture, live stock and bonds has been abandoned in favor of the State income tax. The reason for this was that the tax on personal property was never collected. The local town and county assessors, without investigation, wrote down some small figures opposite each person's name as the assessed valuation of their personal property. In nine cases out of ten the figure did not represent anything like the actual personal property owned. This was especially true in regard to the owners of stocks and bonds, i.e., the richer people of the State, and the result was that the personal property tax was largely evaded by people of means and the burden of it fell on their less fortunate brethren.

I am told that very much the same situation exists in Georgia today; that, for instance, personal property (merchandise) in Atlanta alone is insured for a larger amount than the total assessed value of all the merchandise in the State of Georgia put together. If that is true, your personal property law ought either to be repealed or enforced.

The theory of taxing personal property is, of course, that the State gives it protection and that, therefore, a man should pay in proportion to the amount of personal property which he owns. But the theory is also based on the taxing of all of a man's property, and not merely a small portion thereof. It is undoubtedly true, in this State as in others, not only that the law is not enforced, but that the law itself fails to cover various forms of personal property, such as notes, mortgages, etc., etc.

We need a campaign in Georgia, as in almost every other State, first, for a revision of the tax laws, and, secondly, for their honest and complete enforcement when so revised. It is not stretching the point to state that if all taxes, especially those on property, were enforced 100 per cent, the average man's taxes could be cut from a third to a half.

The unfortunate financial condition of France today is, in very large part, due to the fact that the French taxes are not collected as they should be. The ability of England, with a debt after the war at least as great as that of France, to go back to the gold basis, as was announced the other day, is, in large measure, the result of collecting all of the taxes on her statute books.

A confusion of laws between the Federal and the State governments, an unequal enforcement of those laws, the evasion of many forms of property from taxation altogether, and an unfortunate lack of interest in the subject by the average citizen would make the position of the United States in time of crisis more like that of France than of England.

FRANKLIN D. ROOSEVELT

Warm Springs, Ga.

THE GOOD NEIGHBOR

IN DUTCHESS COUNTY

The Good Neighbor
In Dutchess County

SPEAKING ONE afternoon in 1933 at Poughkeepsie to "my old friends and all neighbors of old Dutchess," Franklin Roosevelt recalled the beginning of his affinity for those people who live near his home at Hyde Park in Dutchess County, New York:

> . . . I want to go back for a minute to the old days before I got to know the United States. It is, I think, just twenty three years ago that I chanced to be in Poughkeepsie on a Saturday morning in August—a very hot Saturday morning.
>
> In front of the court house I ran across a group of friends of mine. As I remember, they were Judge Morchauser, George Spratt, John Mack and Judge Arnold. I had only intended to stay in town for a few minutes to do some errands, but they kidnapped me—one of the first cases of deliberate kidnapping on record—and took me out to the policemen's picnic in Fairview.
>
> On that joyous occasion of clams and sauerkraut and real beer I made my first speech, and I have been apologizing for it ever since.
>
> And also on that same occasion I started to make the acquaintance of that part of Dutchess County that lies outside of the town of Hyde Park.

And I continued to make that acquaintance all through the campaign that year, although in August I hadn't the foggiest idea that I was going to run for the State Senate; and it was only because another band of kidnappers kidnapped me that I got into public life at all.

For I had to talk, and I was given the opportunity of making the acquaintance of a county.

And today, as I drive along a beautiful concrete highway, or one of the new country roads, I see in my mind's eye that same road as it existed in the autumn of 1910 as I proceeded over it at the dangerous pace of about twenty-two miles an hour in Mr. Hawkey's old red Maxwell, without any front windshield, without any top—an old Maxwell that when we met a horse or a team—and that was about every half mile or so—we had to stop, not only the car, but the engine as well.

All through all these succeeding years the friendships that we began at that time have deepened, and, as you know, in spite of absences in Washington and in Albany, I come back to the county on every possible occasion with a true feeling that it is home and that I am once more among my neighbors. . . .

Throughout his mature life, Franklin Roosevelt identified himself intimately with the community about him. It was not simply a personal leaning with him, it was an ancestral pattern. His family had lived in Dutchess County since the French and Indian wars; the land was almost literally the family life. It was a family nourished for many generations in the traditions of the Hudson Valley. For a long time it had had a moderate amount of wealth, which served not to separate the family from the community but to increase its sense of having roots and responsibility in the Valley. There were some outside influences—Mr. Roosevelt's father was sometime Vice-President of the Delaware & Hudson and his maternal grandfather was a China trader who lived out his retirement in the Valley—but the atmosphere of the family was rural, and its feeling for location was in the land. It was this sense that gave Mr. Roosevelt his understanding of people as individuals, his love even of people's names, and his instinct for gauging and working fruitfully with the will of the people. He saw political problems not in terms of disembodied ideologies but in terms of what certain people wanted, what they ought to have, and how other groups of people were likely to feel about it. He had the community sense that people have when they have been in one place for a long time and mean to be there for a long time; he was a Dutchess County citizen who respected his neighbors and meant to get along with them.

It was natural for him as President frequently to reduce the economic and social problems of the country and the world to the simple terms of his Dutchess County background. Often, in conversation, he would explain a point by the experience of some person he knew back in Dutchess. For example, the present writer recalls one evening in 1935 when he was a guest at the White House. The dinner conversation had turned to the subject of the nation's recovery from the depression and Mr. Roosevelt told of a survey conducted at the request of Sir Henri Deterding of the Royal Dutch Shell Company for the purpose of testing the progress of prosperity. The report showed that doctors' bills, grocery bills and so on, were not being paid. "And I understand he had some pretty sensible economists make the survey," the President continued. Mr. Roosevelt agreed that the payment of such bills was likely to be a very good barometer of the trend of prosperity. On the other hand, he did not believe that the survey was accurate. "So, I called in a doctor I know," FDR went on. "He has lived and practiced in the Hudson Valley around Poughkeepsie for thirty years or so. I asked him if he kept accounts. He said he did. I asked him to look up to see how much he had in outstanding debts in March 1933. He reported back to me that in March 1933 he had $3,000 standing out. I asked him how much of that had been paid to date. He told me $2,500. Now, that is progress. That *is* progress," the President repeated.

And in his First Inaugural, Mr. Roosevelt laid down a simple rule of thumb for the country in its relationship to a world made small by air travel and rapid communication:

> In the field of world policy I would dedicate this Nation to the policy of the good neighbor—the neighbor who resolutely respects himself and, because he does so, respects the rights of others—the neighbor who respects his obligations and respects the sanctity of his agreements in and with a world of neighbors.

The community which Franklin Roosevelt instinctively recalled in all such matters had been overwhelmingly Republican for decades, but this did not deter him from his conviction that his Dutchess County neighbors constituted a good cross section of the country and even of the world. In the period between 1858 and 1910, the Dutchess Democrats won a seat in the New York State Senate only once—in 1884. However, in 1910 there was a small but very active group of the Democracy in the county. It was this group, which centered its activities in Poughkeepsie, that chose young FDR to run for the State Senate. The friendships which he made among Democrats and Republicans alike during that successful campaign continued, as he said, all through his life. For example, John Mack was one of the men who started Franklin Roosevelt in politics; and when it came time to nominate him at the Democratic National Convention in 1932, it was John Mack who made the nominating address.

76

Another indication of Mr. Roosevelt's attachment to his neighbors—dating back to his entrance into politics—was the superstitious regularity with which he made his final swing in each political campaign. This trip made on the Monday before Election Day always followed the same pattern—through the towns and counties which had sent him to Albany in that first campaign. So it was that on Monday afternoon, November 6, 1944, the eve of his fourth election to the Presidency, Franklin Roosevelt made what he called "another sentimental journey" among his friends and neighbors in the Hudson Valley. Dressed in a great coat with beaver collar and an old brown campaign fedora, he made the tour through the Republican bailiwick in an open car. The President spoke extemporaneously from his car at Wappingers Falls, Beacon, Newburgh, Kingston and Poughkeepsie. The New York *Times* correspondent reported: "His talks were conversational, neighborly and but rarely touched on major current problems." In her newspaper column, Mrs. Roosevelt commented, "They always stop at the same places, and I think the one in Beacon is where the President made his very first campaign speech when he entered politics as a young man, running in a 'hopeless' district for the State Senate." At least a thousand persons crushed against his car as the motorcade arrived at Bank Square, Beacon. Mr. Roosevelt remarked, on arrival, that he could not speak in Beacon without being introduced by his old friend Morg Hoyt, who had been introducing him "for at least the last 150 years."

Morgan Hoyt and his brother Ferdinand were ardent Democrats from southern Dutchess who had got behind young FDR in his first political race. Morg introduced his neighbor in that first speech of the 1910 campaign and did it pretty regularly thereafter whenever Mr. Roosevelt spoke in that part of the county.

Morg Hoyt began his career as a newspaperman in the 1890's,

when he was a young man in his thirties. From the turn of the century on, Hoyt was a member and frequently chairman of the local Democratic committee. At the time of the 1910 campaign, he was owner and editor of the Matteawan *Journal* which later became the Beacon *Journal* when the towns of Matteawan and Fishkill merged in 1913 to become Beacon. His brother Ferdinand, seventeen years Morgan's junior, was a lawyer, also active in local Democratic politics. In 1910, he was chosen Democratic candidate for the State Assembly to run with FDR and Richard Connell who was seeking the local Congressional seat. In a novel one-month campaign sparked by Mr. Roosevelt and Dick Connell in the red Maxwell, the three of them won their seats.

The Democrats also elected a Governor that year in the nation-wide resurgence against the Taft Administration.

The story is told that on one occasion, FDR and his Maxwell group ran over a farmer's dog. They stopped, went back and offered the farmer five dollars for his loss. The farmer was so amazed by such thoughtfulness (the mortality rate among farmers' chickens and dogs had been quite high along the highways that season) that the Maxwell Democrats got not only this farmer's vote but the vote of at least a dozen more Republicans.

Ferd Hoyt served one term at Albany and was then defeated. He later served several terms as City Judge of Beacon. Hoyt ran for Dutchess County Surrogate in 1926 on a slate fostered by FDR in an attempt to break up the political bosses' clique in the County. He was defeated by the incumbent Republican. Mr. Roosevelt later appointed him New York State Compensation Referee, in which office he served until Thomas E. Dewey became Governor. While serving as referee, Hoyt once ran against Hamilton Fish for Congress and was defeated. In 1920, Hoyt and some associates purchased the Beacon *Journal* from brother Morgan, who continued as editor.

That year the *Journal* had taken on a reporter named Edward T. Hayden, a young man of twenty-two to whom Ferdinand had taken a liking. Hayden turned into a good newspaperman. But toward the middle of the 1920's the going was rough, and the Hoyts sold out to Frank E. Gannett, who merged the paper with the old Fishkill *Herald,* forming the Beacon *News.* As a part of the sale agreement, the Hoyts agreed to stay out of the newspaper business in southern Dutchess for a certain number of years.

In September 1927, Ed Hayden became the publisher of the *Standard,* a weekly published in Southern Dutchess since 1842. It had been a Republican paper up to that time, but Hayden made it a Democratic mouthpiece. Morgan Hoyt was listed on the masthead as editor. While there is no indication in the paper itself that Ferdinand Hoyt figured in its new management, it is fair to surmise that his support was behind it.

At any rate, it was Ferdinand Hoyt who helped young Hayden with one of his more ambitious projects as a publisher. The *Standard* needed money and increased circulation. Hayden and the Hoyts decided on a plan to achieve both. They would get their good friend, fellow Democrat and neighbor, Franklin D. Roosevelt, to become a columnist for the *Standard.* Because of FDR's national stature, increased by his activity for Al Smith at the national convention at Houston, such a column during the Presidential campaign would be sought after by many metropolitan newspapers; it could be syndicated. This plan would fill the paper's coffers and circulation would be increased at the same time.

Mr. Roosevelt returned from Houston early in July. Ferdinand approached him with the plan. He was to write a column for each issue of the *Standard* for the months of August, September, October, up to the election in November—free of charge. According to Hayden's account, FDR welcomed the idea. Morgan Hoyt's version of the story is that the column was conceived upon Roosevelt's return from Houston, that Roosevelt declined at first because he was tired and because he had made commitments to speak in the campaign for Smith. Morgan Hoyt believes that his Hyde Park neighbor was eventually prevailed upon to undertake the additional work because it was suggested he owed it to Al Smith and could thus help Smith in New York State and elsewhere. In any event, both Ed Hayden and Morg Hoyt agree that Ferdinand Hoyt did the negotiating with FDR.

With the prize in his cap, Publisher Hayden went to work. The first notice that he had captured the columnist for *Standard* readers was announced in the issue of July 26, 1928 under the heading "Franklin D. Roosevelt to Write Special Weekly Article for Readers of the *Standard*":

> The Standard is privileged to announce one of the most important and interesting features ever presented to the readers of a Dutchess County newspaper.
>
> Beginning in the issue of next week, August 2, and continuing in each issue thereafter, will be published in the Standard an article on political topics from the pen of Hon. Franklin D. Roosevelt.
>
> These articles will take the form of a regular department in each issue of the Standard and will contain Mr. Roosevelt's comments on the various phases of the presidential campaign and a discussion by him of the issues confronting the voters, considered from the Democratic standpoint.
>
> Franklin D. Roosevelt, Dutchess County's most distinguished son, is today one of the outstanding figures in the National Democratic party.
>
> Mr. Roosevelt's masterly presentation of the arguments in favor of naming of [sic] Governor Smith as the Democratic presidential nominee in his speech at Houston and the consummate skill displayed by him as the Smith floor leader in the convention have attracted nation-wide attention and universal and estimable praise.

And today Franklin D. Roosevelt is looked up to by all factions of the Democracy in all sections of America, and his views on public questions are of prime interest and importance everywhere.

And so, in announcing a regular weekly series of articles by Mr. Roosevelt, written especially for readers of the Standard, we feel that we are presenting a feature of great importance and of compelling interest and which, we believe, will attract wide attention.

During the campaign the Standard will also publish important articles by Henry Morganthau, Jr., another distinguished Dutchess County citizen and publisher of "The American Agriculturist," who will discuss the issues of interest to the farmer, and also important articles by other prominent Democratic leaders.

If you are interested in the issues of the coming presidential campaign, you cannot afford to miss these illuminating features to be presented exclusively to readers of the Standard.

Ed Hayden recalls that FDR prepared the columns for publication in manuscripts typed by Miss LeHand. It was Hayden's custom to pick up the typed manuscript at Hyde Park on Monday mornings. Apparently, the manuscripts have been destroyed; at least neither Hayden nor Morg Hoyt know their present whereabouts.

Roosevelt's column was first printed in the issue of August 2, 1928. It appeared on the first page under the two column head "Between Neighbors" (FDR declared that the column was "addressed primarily to my neighbors in Dutchess County"). The average circulation of the *Standard* during 1928 was about seventeen hundred fifty, and what occurred when the first column appeared is best told by the *Standard's* own account, published August 9, 1928. Readers were advised by the headline: "NEIGHBOR'S COLUMN HAS BIG APPEAL—Widespread Demand for Articles

Written by Franklin D. Roosevelt for the Standard—One Letter Comes by Aeroplane Route—Editors from Maine to California Request Permission to Use Feature Published in Standard." The story ran:

Franklin D.' Roosevelt's column, "Between Neighbors," which is published in the Standard every week, has, as expected, attracted great attention among the newspapers of America, and requests for permission to use the weekly article have been received from the New England States, the South, the corn belt, the Pacific Coast and, in fact, every nook and corner of the United States.

To the editor of the Standard, who secured this popular feature for Dutchess County readers only, it was indeed gratifying when the Associated Press at Albany, a large organization which supplies news to every city in America, asked for the article. Then the New York *Times,* the *Herald-Tribune,* and other metropolitan newspapers asked for the article. Through the Associated Press it was announced throughout the country that The Standard, a small weekly paper in Beacon, was publishing the greatly desired feature. Because Mr. Roosevelt is such an influential national figure, his opinions were sought as much by the Republican *Herald-Tribune* of New York City as by any of the Democratic papers

Immediately after the first of the articles was published, there was a flood of mail in the Standard box at the Beacon Post Office. If the increase continues, it will be necessary to hire one of those bins which Mr. Cummings has reserved in the P. O. building.

Letters came from Georgia, Maine, Mississippi, Florida, Massachusetts, New York, New Jersey, Pennsylvania, Kentucky, Indiana, the Carolinas, Ohio, Minnesota, the Dakotas, and in fact 38 of the United States. The most convincing proof of the universal interest in the paper which bids fair to rival Wm. Allen White's Emporia *Gazette,* was the receipt of a letter from the editor of the *Bee,* a newspaper in Fresno, California. This letter was sent by Air Mail (postage only 12 cents). It was mailed from the Pacific Coast on Friday, August 3rd, addressed to The Standard, New York City. The ever alert U. S. Postal force caught the error and the letter was delivered through the Beacon Post Office on Tuesday afternoon.

The Fresno *Bee* and hundreds of other newspapers learned through the Associated Press that the Standard was carrying important comment upon the developments of the campaign. The Editor of the *Bee* wrote, "Please send issues of your paper containing Franklin D. Roosevelt's articles.

If you will send bill, it will be taken care of immediately." Out in Indiana, John Isenberger, prominent editor, writes as follows—"I have noticed in the newspapers that Franklin D. Roosevelt is writing articles for The Standard under the caption 'Between Neighbors'. I would appreciate it very much if you would send your paper with these articles. I am for Al Smith and believe he has a good chance to carry Indiana."

From Des Moines, Iowa, came a request from five citizens who had read the story in the Burlington *Hawkeye* and want to receive every issue of the Standard in which an article written by Mr. Roosevelt appears.

Many persons who are former residents of Beacon and read the important announcement from Beacon also wrote the editor of the Standard. Of these a typical letter was received from Frank Ferrone, former Beacon boy who has an insurance office of his own in Washington, D. C. He writes, "I am glad to see that the Standard is putting Beacon on the map. I read the enclosed article in the Washington *Post*, and now I am able to convince my friends down here that there is such a place as Beacon." Mr. Ferrone sent the clipping from the Washington *Post*, one of the largest papers in the national capital.

Hundreds of other letters were also received from various parts of the country, after the many papers which have the Associated Press service printed the first of the series of articles by Mr. Roosevelt, a former State Senator and former Assistant Secretary of the U. S. Navy.

Turning to the editorial page, one finds the editor of the *Standard* enjoying his success further as he comments in an editorial entitled "Widespread Attention":

> The nation-wide attention the articles which are being published in the Standard from the pen of Franklin D. Roosevelt are receiving shows in how high esteem this leading Dutchess County citizen is held by all classes.
> We do not believe there is a man in the Democratic party who commands the respect of all classes as does Mr. Roosevelt. And when he speaks or writes, he has the happy faculty of emphasizing in a nice way his telling points.
> Mr. Roosevelt's articles in the Standard seem destined to play an important part in the campaign.

One of the Republican leaders in Dutchess was a distinguished Beacon lawyer, Vincent D. Stearns. Taking up FDR's statement in his first column: "that he hoped Mr. Hayden would get some Republican to write each week in this paper," Stearns addressed the following letter to the *Standard*:

> The "Between Neighbors" column in The Standard, by Mr. Franklin D. Roosevelt, is an admirably conceived idea. Some one of the 'Neighbors' might well follow his suggestion and make friendly reply.
> The first article is of particular interest as a possible indication of what may be expected in the series, and Mr. Roosevelt having selected a Beacon paper as the vehicle for his opinions, perhaps it would not be too presumptuous if a Beacon 'neighbor' became sufficiently interested to break into print. I am, therefore, submitting this paper for use; unless someone, with more political weight than I, takes up the wager.

I have seen Mr. Roosevelt on several occasions, and talked with him and heard him talk. I was among those present last Fall when he entertained the so-called "Pilgrimage" of the Dutchess County Historical Society at his country home, so that I have some knowledge of the man and his home environment—also his courage.

It is my feeling that the newspaper reporters who stated, in substance, that Mr. Roosevelt was by far the finest thing in the Houston convention, were not overly fulsome in their praise. We Republicans among his "neighbors" respect him, and regret that his convictions are such that he must be opposed to us politically. Otherwise, he is a good neighbor.

We have very little "bitter partisanship" in Dutchess County. The voters seem to have decidedly independent ideas regarding whom we will support and we divide most noticeably at Presidential elections.

After the introduction, the balance of Mr. Roosevelt's article discusses only the K.K.K. and Senator Heflin. Something is also said about bigots. Without doubt, they do exist and they are found in every race and sect. It is also possible that Senator Heflin, as Mr. Roosevelt says, created a realization of this. I cannot conceive of fashions in bigotry however, and describing bigotry as "old fashioned" can only result in resurrecting cadavers which have been dead and buried for hundreds of years.

I did not hear Senator Heflin's Dutchess County Speech, but they tell me that the crowd was far from a record one and that the applause was very slight and enthusiasm lacking. No doubt, as Mr. Roosevelt says, "the large majority went to hear him out of sheer curiosity." That being so in Dutchess County, New York, and, according to Mr. Roosevelt, "It (the Klan) has since nearly died out" in Georgia, and as Mr. Roosevelt assumes his neighbors to be a representative cross section of the county, where is the necessity and why should he say that "the time has come to prove definitely that it (bigotry) must not and cannot

85

be a controlling factor in our national life." Of course it must not, and of course it cannot—it never has.

There are a great many people, independent, straightforward, free thinking, Republicans and Democrats, who are solid citizens and who, in a general way, have a kindly feeling toward all men, and have been moderately inoculated with the commandment—"Love Thy Neighbor as Thyself." A too strong inoculation has been known to result in the paternalism of meddling. Perhaps this type of "neighbor" forms the vast majority. It is a waste of time to argue with a bigot, no matter in what camp he belongs. I am somewhat like the member of the Georgia Chamber of Commerce mentioned by Mr. Roosevelt in that I know so many creeds, and have so many friends of sterling character among all classes, that the charge and countercharge is not worrying me at all. Most people are not something else because their parents happen to be what they are. It is all rather confusing.

In fact, not so much was heard of the K.K.K. politically until the issue was used as a football at the 1924 Democratic Convention. It split the Democratic party wide open then so far as the convention was concerned. The last four years seem to have healed the wound so that the scar is very light.

The K.K.K., bigotry or religion are not, either singly or together, issues in this campaign and if they are, Senator Heflin, who is a Democrat, and Mr. Roosevelt, who is a Democrat, and all the rest of the Democrats who are starting to talk these issues are the Democratic Party, must be responsible for the dirty work.

Just why Mr. Roosevelt makes bigotry and religion the topic of his first article in this political series, is not understandable.

The danger of this issue is with the fair minded man I have tried to picture. He wants to be fair and a good sport so hard that he will lean over backwards to do it. We then have the possibility and probability—under the ballyhoo of the Democratic party regarding religious persecutions—

86

that he will vote for Al Smith to show that he is not a bigot, but a fair, independent, straight shooter. The result of this is that Al Smith gains a vote instead of losing one because of this Democratic religion and bigotry issue, and that is exactly the frame of mind which the Democratic organization is trying to create among independent Republican voters.

Is it possible that there are enrolled Republicans who will vote for Al Smith because their ideas and ideals of religions are alike? If so, can it not be just as strongly urged that Herbert Hoover is being persecuted because he is a Quaker? There is one of the smaller sects of Christendom, noted for its peacefulness and love of its neighbors.

We don't care anything about this old issue which split the Democratic party of 1924. We are going to vote for Herbert Hoover because, among other things, he is every inch a man. Starting in life as a blacksmith's son, by his own efforts and without political connections or assistance, he has climbed his way to world wide recognition as a master executive of national affairs. Let every voter vote for the man and party he thinks best equipped mentally, morally and in the theory of government to continue our long sustained prosperity, and let us all forget the non-existent "old-fashioned" ideas of bigots.

Quickly coming to the defense of its columnist, the *Standard* replied editorially to Stearns:

In this issue of the Standard there appears a letter written by our estimable friend, Vincent D. Stearns, former corporation counsel of the City of Beacon, in which he takes Franklin D. Roosevelt, Dutchess County's most prominent son, to task for his mention of the visit of Senator Heflin to Dutchess County. The fact is well known that Senator Heflin, an ardent Democrat, has been traveling about the country making speeches and he has only one subject. It has been a popular subject with his audiences. Mr. Stearns does not commend the policy of Mr. Heflin, nor does he give credit for the fair, honest, open and above-board manner in which Mr. Roosevelt handled the delicate subject. He did not discuss it with any idea of bringing in a new issue, nor of creating ill feeling among religious groups in any community in America. He wrote with the idea of creating that true spirit of "Peace On Earth, Good Will To Men."

The letter of Mr. Stearns was written in all sincerity, and we are glad to publish it, but we would ask readers to consider the contrast with the written statements in Mr. Roosevelt's column, "Between Neighbors." He cited an incident in his own life to show the fallacy of ill feeling over religion, and he did it in such a way that it brought letters from all over this country of ours, commending him upon his fairness. As Mr. Roosevelt so well said in concluding that column, "Think It Over."

The New York *Times* took cognizance of Mr. Roosevelt's newspaper venture by devoting a full column to reprinting his first article. The *Times* story, captioned "F. D. Roosevelt Turns Columnist," attracted the attention of at least one reader who was moved to comment in a letter to the editor of the *Standard*:

> Referring to Mr. Roosevelt's column Between Neighbors, published in your paper recently, as quoted in the N. Y. Times, I hope you will allow the space in your valued weekly for the expression of my opinion, an opinion which I believe is shared by a considerable number in your own community, and by quite a few whose name is legion throughout the State and Nation.
>
> While Mr. Roosevelt's preachment on Tolerance is altogether admirable in a general way, he is laboring under a tremendous illusion if he imagines that because the constitution guarantees religious liberty, it constitutes a valid reason for the citizenry of these United States to vote for Al Smith, a devout Catholic (so he declared himself), for the highest office in the land.

Were Mr. Roosevelt to consider the Constitutional precept in its proper light, I doubt very much if he would have mentioned it in this connection. For no one in this great Country of ours, not even Senator Heflin, questions the right of religious liberty. The question at issue is simply this: Should a Catholic, a devout Catholic as Al Smith is, be chosen as the head of our nation?

Imagine for a moment a Catholic in the White House and the Mexican problem still unsolved. "How could a President make war?" you say. Well, a President of the U. S. A. has enormous powers. He need not figure in any such thing directly, but he can, calculatingly, scatter substantial sparks in certain high explosive places and the firebrands complete the trick. Do we want more war? Do we want any religious wars?

The Catholic church, despite its American disclaimer, is ruled from without. Its supreme head is a foreigner, living in a foreign land, yet Catholics the world over faithfully believe him the highest authority on earth. It is not a question of being legally bound, but instinctively every devout Catholic is pledged to obey him. This highest authority (so called) considers all persons outside his church as infidels, faithless and full of error. It is a fact that the Catholic church has ever been craving for power. Right or otherwise it is always in the firm belief that it can do no wrong. Do we want any member of this menacing organization to occupy the very greatest position in our national life?

I refer to the Catholic church as a menacing organization advisedly. It is even here and now a menace to our institutions. The spread of its Parochial schools alone is sufficient to brand it as absolutely un-American and decidedly alien. Think of it, our great Public Schools and Universities are not good enough for the Catholics. They prefer that appalling black garb of the nunneries which fills every sensitive eye with terror. Who knows but that the Pope may some day issue an encyclical ordering all women, young and those who can still manage to appear young, to wear this frightful style. Rascob, a life-long Republican, turns overnight a Democrat because of a special dispensation.

And how does Al Smith personally measure up in fitness for the great and high office of the Presidency? Everyone knows that his education is exceedingly limited. His political training, at most, local. He may know his sidewalks, but it can hardly be assumed that he is even familiar with the open roads and highways of our country. The Prohibition question is merely a blind. There are far more important things than whiskey or McGinnis stout. On most of the greater problems Al remains incommunicado. Who really expects him to know these things?

In so far as our own Empire State is concerned people around here have never been much impressed with his so-called reforms, or the good they have accomplished. Recently, for effect, he ordered an investigation of the Gas and Electricity merger. Rascob will no doubt extend them an invitation to subscribe. Did Al ever before make any effort to investigate the exorbitant prices exacted from the people by these very companies who have merged? The same inactivity on his part applies to all the other Public Service corporations. Some years ago a former Governor successfully stopped Race Track gambling and thus protected the people. Did Al during his four terms in Albany ever make a try to stop gambling in the greatest gambling hell in the world—the N. Y. Stock Exchange? He is a shrewd politician, to be very sure; he signed certain bills rather quickly despite the fact that a Commission appointed by him advised against it.

Quotes Mr. Roosevelt: "Love thy neighbor as thyself." Well, Ecclesiastes says somewhere: To everything there is a season, a time to love and a time to hate. Tolerance is indeed an outstanding virtue in our nation. The very fact that untold numbers of Catholics, Jews, etc. are occupying positions of importance proves this conclusively. However,

Mr. Roosevelt gives himself away completely when he tells the story of his about that Chamber of Commerce meeting in Georgia, a KKK organization having a Catholic as secretary and a Jew a director. Very obviously, the President of that Club was a good and tolerant Protestant. He knew those men so it was all right enough. By the same token, this should be exactly the reason why good Americans, be they Catholics or Jews, should not vote for a Catholic for President. It is by far more safe to elect the same type of men as those before them who have labored to make this country what it is.

Let Mr. Roosevelt think it over.

FDR'S second column, on the factors in modern American life tending to decrease the numbers of misinformed or unreasoning voters, brought Mr. Stearns to pen and ink once more. Without comment, the *Standard* published his rebuttal August 16th:

In the early dawn of political history, the selections of the heads of the "hundreds" or clans were made at public meetings attended by all of the voters. We have, again, witnessed an approach to this, by means of the radio; and the entire nation will hear the nominations of the candidates and so determine their personality and sincerity, so far as their manner and speech may convey it.

We have, indeed, broken down the barriers of distance, and the old-fashioned campaign, whether by automobile or buggy, such as Mr. Roosevelt describes, has, in that short period of eighteen years, become ancient history and a thing of the past. Education and political enlightenment are widespread. A man need not necessarily be the proud possessor of a college degree, or even high school education, to have acquired through the years that good hard common sense and fine judgment of material things which is the characteristic of the masses of our country. Schooling, of course, is of wonderful assistance to every man enjoying it, but it does not follow the man without schooling may not be competent to make correct decisions, politically. Mr. Roosevelt mentions Henry Ford as a benefactor of our country; and it has been said that Mr. Ford lacks somewhat in schooling, and that instead of knowing history he makes it. There are all manners and degrees of competent intelligence from Mr. Ford down to the apprentice in his factory, and they are all capable of sifting out the good and bad from whisperings.

Mr. Roosevelt, so far, has refrained from making any direct charges, but has referred and hinted at various things, and is now referring to whispering campaigns, and voters who are bound by a party collar. This reference must be connected up with statements in other official Democratic publications, and the New York *World,* in one of its issues shortly preceding Mr. Roosevelt's last article, inquires whether Herbert Hoover will want to profit by the votes which he may gain by reason of the whisperings against Alfred E. Smith. Does Mr. Roosevelt consider such campaigning as that to be "fair"?

Everybody knows that there is no organized or disorganized or any other kind of effort or intention by any Republican organizations to circulate any of these so-called whisperings. Mr. Roosevelt says that there are whisperings against Herbert Hoover as much as there are whisperings against Alfred E. Smith, and that they always whisper against everyone in political office as well as their families. I have yet to hear any Republican papers complaining about these whisperings, or trying to make it appear that Mr. Smith is responsible for whisperings against Mr. Hoover. You cannot stop the "neighbors" from talking. "Talk is cheap." They don't mean half of it, and no one is responsible for it.

Nevertheless, these charges of whisperings are all a part and parcel of the effort to reach the result which I tried to outline last week, and such efforts are responsible party policies. If the independent fairminded voter can be made to believe that Alfred E. Smith is not being treated fairly, and that somebody (particularly the Republican party) is persecuting him, and these accusations create a sympathy, why then, perhaps, some of our independent, fair-minded voters will become sorry for him and, in their pity, they will vote for him.

Mr. Roosevelt's remarks about having a life job bring to mind this thought. President Coolidge at the end of his first elective term did not "choose" to run again, even though he was, at the close of the term, possibly the most popular president this country has ever known, and would without question have been re-elected. Alfred E. Smith has campaigned and talked his way into four terms as governor of the State of New York. Does it seem probable that he would be willing to follow the unwritten law of no third term, or does it seem more probable that, if once he got in, he would be there to stay as long as the political machine, which Tammany patronage would build up, could keep him there?

The voters are not to be misled by manufactured sympathies. What about the men, the platforms and the issues, Mr. Roosevelt?

Insofar as an examination of the files of the *Standard* reveals, everything went along quietly for a few weeks. There were no published comments about the column by readers and no *Standard* editorials on the subject. Undoubtedly, some of this tranquillity was due to the fact Stearns was on a vacation—about which the readers learned upon seeing the *Standard* for September 13, 1928, where, in "The Letter Box," this communication appeared:

Upon return from vacation I find Mr. Roosevelt wrestling with the Farm Relief problem. He divided the match into two falls, losing the first; and I cannot see how he can possibly win the second.

The problem of Farm Relief is with us, and is one of the most difficult and technical problems facing the country today. The actual problem is not a political issue, but the methods and theories for relief held by the two candidates are issues. Governor Smith, to date, has gone both ways. In August he was for the equalization fee, and in September he is against it, and he now promises by his first western speech to tell the country exactly what his theory is. It is very plain that he has no theory for actual relief, but hopes to gain some votes if he can strike the popular cord among the western farmers. This shilly-shallying and clear lack of knowledge and purpose ought to cost him every farmer's vote. How can New York side-walks KNOW about farm problems anyway?

I am impressed with the possibility of only two theories for Farm Relief; the first of which was fairly set forth by the Farm Relief Bill, vetoed by President Coolidge during the last Congress, and which contained the equaliza-tion fee theory now pestering Governor Smith. In this theory there would be a law creating a bureau and com-pelling every farmer in the country to operate his farm and sell his produce pursuant to the provisions and restrictions of that law. Such a law would necessitate a vast force of federal employees to carry out the operation of the law and regulate the farms, and to spy upon and prosecute those farmers who did not live up to and comply with it.

There is another theory which is the one adopted by the Republican party and Herbert Hoover, its candidate, and that is that a thorough investigation of conditions be made and such legislation passed as will permit farmers or groups of farmers to avail themselves of the privileges conferred by this legislation, and to so cooperate in the raising and marketing of their produce and the financing of their endeavors that the farms may be operated at a profit.

There are now, in this country, approximately one gov-ernmental employee to every ten citizens, and the end is not in sight. Under the first theory this vast army of pub-lic employees would be materially increased; under the second theory there would be comparatively few additional employees.

Since the advent of chain stores, thousands of small business men have been forced out of competition, and it is only recently that combinations have been made by those still remaining for the purpose of cooperative buying and merchandising. Yet, legislation for the protection of the retail grocer, butcher, cigar store and drug store would seem rather absurd to the average voter, and I am impressed with the possible truth of the contention that one of the great difficulties in farms today is the competition from the huge operations in the western states. It is certain that the agriculturist in this part of the country does not want, and in fact is very much against, the so-called Farm Relief.

Under the Democratic and Smith theory of Farm Relief, the farmer will be forced by law, under threat of police, arrest, prosecution, fine and imprisonment, to operate and merchandise his farm pursuant to that law. Another unpopular law with evasion and corruption.

Under the Republican and Hoover theory of Farm Relief, the farmer will be given an opportunity to choose whether he will take advantage of such government assistance in cooperative buying and merchandising and financial help as a careful and serious study and survey of the difficulties may show to be for his greatest benefit.

In mid-September, Mr. Roosevelt's newspaper stint began to conflict with his obligations as a speaker for Al Smith in the Presidential campaign and with his own desire to spend some time at Warm Springs. Hence, he wrote two post-dated columns to give himself a breather in which to do these other things. Accordingly, at the time he prepared his column for the September 20th issue—the column dated at Hyde Park, September 15, 1928—FDR advised his publisher of this fact. Among the numerous personal letters from Mr. Roosevelt to his old friend Morg Hoyt there is what appears to be the bottom part of a letter in FDR's handwriting:

I am off on Monday for Warm Springs, Georgia, to be gone for two weeks—address me there if anything turns up.

I have prepared two other articles and will send them in a few days.

Sincerely,

F. D. ROOSEVELT

The two articles referred to are undoubtedly those dated at Hyde Park, September 22nd and September 29th, published in the *Standard* on September 27th and October 4th, respectively.

Mr. Roosevelt left Hyde Park about September 20th, and the ensuing two weeks turned out to be eventful for him. In a note near the beginning of the first volume of his *Public Papers,* he has summarized the fortnight for us:

I was nominated by the Democratic State Convention at Rochester on October 3, 1928. I accepted the nomination only after very urgent persuasion by Governor Alfred E. Smith, who was at that time campaigning as the Democratic candidate for the Presidency of the United States.

During the Rochester convention I was in Warm Springs, continuing my treatment for infantile paralysis, and my doctors had strongly advised me against reentering public life at that time. It was against their advice and largely because of the thought that I could be of service in promoting the cause of liberal and progressive government in the State and, through the election of Governor Smith, in the Nation, that I finally yielded.

Before my campaign for the Governorship began I had made several speeches in behalf of the candidacy of Governor Smith for the Presidency. Included among these were speeches at Atlanta, Ga., September 26, 1928; Manchester, Ga., October 2, 1928; Columbus, Ga., October 5, 1928; Cleveland, Ohio, October 6, 1928; Boston, Mass., October 12, 1928; New York City, October 15, 1928.

Neighbor Roosevelt had scarcely received the nomination of his party for the Governorship when, on October 4th, the *Standard* proudly stated in a news story confidently entitled, "Governor Not Too Busy for Article." It boasted that FDR had found time to write his weekly article for the *Standard* despite the fact that he was "making speeches all over the country and has been very busy the past week making up his mind whether he will accede to the demands of thousands to accept the nomination for Governor." The *Standard's* enthusiasm was not embarrassed by the slight inaccuracy: it is clear now that Mr. Roosevelt had written the article in question several days before he went South and was prevailed upon by Al Smith to accept the Democratic leadership of New York State. The *Standard* was boasting not about itself but about its friend and champion.

On his return to Hyde Park, Candidate Roosevelt was confronted with the job of shaping and carrying out his own campaign as well as making several more speeches for Al Smith. Slowly broadening responsibilities were disturbing the tranquillity of the Dutchess countryside. These responsibilities would not wait for Mr. Roosevelt's complete convalescence; they would surely not wait for the articles which he had promised Ferdinand Hoyt. The little corner in which there had been this quiet talking "between neighbors" had slowly widened; private walls dissolved, county lines faded into state lines, but these lines were fading too, and soon the talk would be to a nation. And so Ed Hayden recalls that Miss LeHand telephoned him about the time the column for the October 11th issue should have been ready and told him that Mr. Roosevelt would have to discontinue the column because Al Smith had asked him to run for Governor, and this would require a stumping tour throughout the state. There would be no time for the weekly article. Nevertheless, the two column box headed "Between Neighbors," appeared in the October 11th *Standard,* and its editor, bowing good-naturedly despite his disappointment, wrote:

> For the first time in several weeks the Standard does not carry the special feature article written exclusively for this paper by Franklin D. Roosevelt, Democratic candidate for Governor.
>
> Every reader of the Standard knows the reason for this, and we are sure they will appreciate the fact that, for the first time, Mr. Roosevelt was unable to continue his weekly chats to his neighbors in Dutchess County through the medium of this paper.
>
> However, residents of Dutchess County, Democrats and Republicans alike, fully realize that the gubernatorial nominee is extremely busy this week, and, for the purpose of continuing the "Between Neighbors" column, which has become so popular because of the admiration which citizens of Dutchess County have for her most distinguished son, we take this occasion of thanking the many Republicans who have already expressed to us their intentions of voting for Mr. Roosevelt.
>
> It is indeed gratifying to all residents of Dutchess County casting aside political affiliations to show their confidence in the man who so ably represented this district in the United States [sic] Senate and who had a remarkable record as Assistant Secretary of the Navy during the great World War.
>
> Morgan H. Hoyt, chairman of the city committee of Beacon, is making efforts to have Mr. Roosevelt speak in Beacon before the campaign closes. Originally, it was arranged that Mr. Roosevelt would speak in Beacon during the closing week of the campaign, but he was nominated as the candidate for Governor so unexpectedly that his plans have been altered because of necessity. However, it is safe to say that our distinguished neighbor will pay a

visit to Beacon before he winds up his campaign and Beacon will undoubtedly pay him the greatest tribute which has ever been accorded a candidate for office.

Candidate Roosevelt carried on a whirlwind campaign around the state. The best record of it is found in the first volume of his *Public Papers* where all his major speeches are printed. Throughout the campaign, the *Standard* printed news stories and editorials on the progress of its columnist in his race for the Governorship. After closing his campaign in Madison Square Garden on the previous Saturday, FDR made his usual Monday-before-election swing through the valley towns. The *Standard* welcomed both its hero and its neighbor in the boast that Franklin Roosevelt was "coming back to the spot where he made his first political speech." And the New York *Times* for November 6, 1928, recorded the event:

> Leaving his home at Hyde Park this morning the candidate drove to Beacon where he was met by a band and an automobile procession that escorted him to Bank Square where 2,000 persons were waiting. Introduced by Ferdinand Hoyt, chairman of the reception committee, the nominee told his listeners that he hoped he would receive the same support from Beacon as was given him in 1910 when he made a successful campaign for the State Senate.
>
> His address was informal and neighborly rather than political, since he said he considered his campaign closed with the Madison Square Garden meeting on Saturday night.

It is now familiar history that Al Smith lost his home State to Herbert Hoover, but that Roosevelt went into the Governor's chair with a plurality of about 25,000 votes. True to form, Hyde Park and Dutchess County were a bulwark of Republican strength, and Neighbor Franklin did not carry his home town or county. His partisan, the *Standard,* published an indignant editorial on the subject:

99

The vote of Hyde Park, Dutchess County, has been the subject of much discussion, since the returns of Tuesday's election were made known. When Franklin D. Roosevelt ran for the office of Vice-President, he lost his own district in Hyde Park in the election. How [sic]—nothing unusual about that. The voter is required to vote for the Vice-President on the same ticket as his choice for President. For that reason, Mr. Roosevelt did not receive the votes of many Republicans in Hyde Park in that election. However, there was no excuse this year for the residents to show their opposition to their fellow townsman, who was nominated by a major political party as their candidate for the highest honor within the gift of the people of New York State. Early in the campaign it was reported that many prominent Republicans in Hyde Park had contributed to the fund for a Roosevelt banner in that community. It appears that the town felt honored, but when the time to show confidence in the man who has done much for the community arrived, the citizens were lacking. Palo Alto and West Branch both claimed Herbert Hoover as a native son, gave him pluralities which were overwhelming. Hyde Park could have done the same without the slightest effect on the outcome of the election.

Dutchess County should be ashamed of Hyde Park. Beacon, in the southern extremity of the county, gave the candidate for Governor a much better demonstration of neighborliness. While Mr. Smith lost the city by 457 votes, Mr. Roosevelt was only defeated by 211. Many Republicans who would have voted for him as a neighbor failed to do so for fear of spoiling their ballots, or he would have carried the city. If Beacon had the honor of having such a distinguished son, our vote for him would have been almost unanimous, regardless of his political belief.

Franklin Roosevelt's chats "Between Neighbors" thus ended in what was, for the moment, something of a paradox in neighborliness. He had carried his state, but not Hyde Park. It might be that the Hyde Park vote reflected on the candidate but not the man—for it was once said that in spite of the fact that they voted against him, all his neighbors loved him. But in any case, the point of literal fact lost importance as Mr. Roosevelt's destined neighborhood steadily widened. He had addressed his column to his neighbors; not his neighbors but a whole state had responded. And those horizons, too, were already melting into new distances. It was as if the quiet voice over a Dutchess County fence had been picked up unaware by a battery of microphones. In a few short years that same quiet, reassuring voice would be heard at the firesides of an entire nation, from end to end, in those words with which it came to be identified: "My friends." It would soon speak to a world, bringing courage and hope of deliverance, but essentially the same message which it had brought to Dutchess County: that we are neighbors. The columns that follow are almost prophetic in their anxiety about bigotry and narrowness. It happened that they were concerned with a specific campaign issue, but soon the author would apply the same humaneness and understanding to a tormented world, bringing to all peoples the hope that one day they might all live together as neighbors.

In this deep sense, the columns ended in no paradox, but in the richest possible fulfillment. Robert Maynard Hutchins once said that we have neighbors in time as well as in space. Franklin Roosevelt, in these columns as in his life-work, speaks to us and— beyond us—to them.

COLUMNS

IN

THE STANDARD

1928

THE STANDARD

THE SOUTHERN DUTCHESS COUNTY WEEKLY NEWSPAPER

$2.00 Per Year   FISHKILL & BEACON, DUTCHESS COUNTY, N. Y., THURSDAY, AUGUST 2, 1928.

A
ub Here
t Monday

ted To Attend
g On That
ing

TERS OPEN
ST OF WEEK

Men Plan To
Notification

ar of headquarters
ion formerly had
e Bernstein Block
the city, the local
be said to be un-

sbinson be ner will
on within a day or
bled and the rooms
he greater part of
r election.

undred signatures
ned for the men's
the women are also
atisfactorily.

the forming of an
Men's Club will be
at the rooms. Of-
ed and preliminary
ttending the notifi-
s be held in Albany
August 22.

that later in the
ning of the follow-
aplete the organiza-
a club. It is hoped
n speakers at this

Operation

2, Stanley Beat, of
re in Beacon over
visit Mr. Beat's
erwent a serious
office of Dr. An-
rs. Beat has been
affliction of the
ars, and the defec-
n was removed by
ed by Dr. George

ARD LUCK

aployees of a diner
ought he would try
ug this week, so
erythin' he went to
o boat was procur-
d soda water stored
a few feet from
mber of the family
into the lake. That
as she was obliged
change of cloth'g.

BETWEEN NEIGHBORS

I am glad to have a chance to be an occasional "colyumnist" in "The Standard" this summer and autumn, and Will Rogers, Heywood Broun and F. P. A. will have to look out. My remarks, however, will be more or less serious, and are addressed primarily to my neighbors in Dutchess County.

These neighbors of mine are a representative cross-section of the community, and are made up of Republicans, Democrats and people who are not affiliated with any party. Therefore in talking about poli- tics, I am keeping that fact in mind and have no intention of using the shop worn methods of condemning everything on one side and praising everything on the other side of the political fence.

The day has gone by when you can fool people into believing that the nation, or a state or a county — a city is going to the dogs just be- cause one political party happens to be in power in it. People are sick of the kind of editorial writing which sees only good in every measure and every man sponsored by one party and only bad on the other side. So, too, it is the little provincial papers that today in the news-columns magnify as first page news any disagreement in their opponents' camps and run only a half inch on the back page about any trouble in their own camp.

That is one reason why the bitterly partisan press is losing its in- fluence in this country. The other reason is that there is more and better education everywhere and readers do not as much as formally take the views and news of a one sided paper as Gospel Truth. I told Mr. Hayden I hoped he would not permit everything to write each week in this paper, but if he can't find one, I shall try to be as fair as I can.

Take as an example this visit of Senator Heflin to make a speech in Dutchess County. The Senator had a legal right to speak and prob- ably the large majority of his audience went to hear him out of sheer curiosity. Probably no man in the United States has done more to help the nomination of, and increase the support for Governor Smith all over this country than Senator Heflin.

He has made the nation realize that old fashioned bigotry does exist, a little of it in every section and a lot of it in some places and that the time has come to prove definitely that it must not and cannot be a controlling factor in our national life.

Here is a story about the Ku Klux Klan that could almost be call- ed a Parable—but it is a true story and happened to me.

Three years ago I was the guest of honor at a Chamber of Com- merce Banquet in a small city in Georgia. It was a community of al- most pure Scotch and English Protestant ancestry. I sat on the right of the Mayor of the Town and on the other side of me sat the Secre- tary of the Chamber of Commerce, a young man born in Italy, and a Roman Catholic. Just beyond sat a Jew who was a member of the Executive Committee.

I turned to the Mayor and asked him if the Ku Klux Klan was strong in the city. He said "Yes, very." (It has since then nearly died out). Then I asked if most of the members of the Chamber belonged to the Klan, and again he said "yes".

Then I said "If that is so, why is it that the Secretary is a Catholic and that a Jew is on the Executive Committee?"

He turned to me utterly surprised and answered: "Why, Mr. Roosevelt, we know those men. They are intimate friends of ours, we respect them and like them. You know this Klan business doesn't ap- ply to people you know!"

I often wonder if those unfortunates who are working in open de- fence of that article of the Constitution of the United States which guarantees religious liberty are also opposed to the great command- ment "Thou shalt love thy neighbor as thyself."

Think it over.

July 30, 1928.

FRANKLIN D. ROOSEVELT.

GET CONTRACT FOR A PUTNAM COUNTY ROAD

The awarding of the Haviland Hollow road in Putnam County was awarded at Carmel on Monday. The Shackett-Scofield Inc. concern were awarded the contract.

The road runs from the Patterson Brewster road near Patterson to the Connecticut line. The distance is about three miles.

Incidentally, it is the route Harry Thaw took to get across the line when he made his sensational escape from Matteawan.

Get Big Contract

Harry and Macy, structural iron workers, have recently been award- ed a large contract on a new modern brickyard to be erected in Newton Hook for the Empire Brick and Sup- ply Co. Nearly a dozen contractors submitted estimates on the work, but the Beacon firm was successful, and their experience in work of this na- ture was taken into consideration, as they had done the iron work on Denning's Point plant, which is the finest along the Hudson. Work on the contract will get under way in the middle of September. Skilled mechanics will be taken to Newton Hook and laborers will be employed there.

Complain Of Roads

Campers in this section who have occasion to use the Beacon streets are complaining every day about their condition, and many of the campers who drive automobiles are quoted as saying that they will go elsewhere for their recreation in the future.

BOARD OF EDUCATION MET THE ARCHITECT

The members of the Board of Edu- cation met the Architect at the new South Avenue school site a few days ago and went over the plans with him.

The work is now proceeding very satisfactorily.

STANLEY TO ENTERTAIN

Archie Stanley noted entertainer, now home on his vacation, will en- tertain at the Strand Theatre, Nel- sonville Saturday evening.

TRANSFER OF PROPERTY

K. John Jakubiel has sold his property at 25 Prospect Place to Su- san Pompa. The sale was made through the agency of William Nich- olson.

A FINE LINE

When doing your shopping in town, don't forget that Doc Henry

GUEST OF CANADA

Pete Lynch has left town to be the guest of Canada for a week. He does not leave town very often, hence

PETER J. LYNCH

the trip is of unusual news value. When the staff photographer of the Standard took this snot of Mr. Lynch as he was departing he was carry- ing his valise in one hand and his handbag in the other, and they did not get into the picture.

Mr. Lynch confided to a Standard representative that he hasn't been out of Beacon many times in a quarter of a century. His must re- cent trip was to Troy last year. On that occasion he went by train and took out accident insurance for a large sum to insure his safe return to Beacon.

On his motor trip through the New England States and Canada Mr. Lynch is accompanied by James Tynn, Harold Brilliant and Michael O'Malley, who carried the old reli- able black bag when he departed.

Phil Vanderburgh is taking care of Mr. Lynch's Tom Cat during his absence.

TO FORM CLUB

There will be a meeting of everyone in Beacon irrespective of party affiliation who favor the election of Alfred E. Smith as president, at the Democratic Headquarters rooms in the east end of the city, formerly occu- pied by the Salvation Army in the Bernstein Block, on Monday evening next at 8 o'clock.

Officers are to be elected, some plans laid for the notification exercises at Al- bany and other plans for the campaign outlined.

It is hoped to have a speaker present. Everyone who favors

INTERE FEA WI

In this issue is an article b velt which will attention Mr the outstanding his opinions ar importance I already unde Since it was Standard's new velt was to joi Standard on a pers in New Y Standard has these papers re to use the wee Mr. Roosevelt of the general i first of whi sue of the Sta exclusive rights is to be known bors". If you with the devel paign as seen n men of Americ velt's column Standard.

General Clea At

Announcement eral clearance linery at the E All our to make ro play. In this c the most beauti aid your eyes o marked far belo Some of these are less than they wholesale.

It is a great o vacation needs occasion. 'See where in the S

ALSO AT

The clearance at the Pearson This store carri line as the Beac prices will pre clearance

It's hard worth son who is willing of an argument.

In a calm Se —German.

An Where you ca must creep und

He who bo boasts of what h ers.

An angry

I

"The Day Has Gone By When You Can Fool People Into Believing the Nation Is Going to the Dogs Just Because One Political Party Happens to Be in Power"

Thursday, August 2, 1928

I AM glad to have a chance to be an occasional "colyumn-ist" in "The Standard" this summer and autumn, and Will Rogers, Heywood Broun and F.P.A. will have to look out. My remarks, however, will be more or less serious, and are addressed primarily to my neighbors in Dutchess County.

These neighbors of mine are a representative cross-section of the community, and are made up of Republicans, Democrats and people who are not affiliated with any party. Therefore in talking about politics, I am keeping that fact in mind and have no intention of using the shop-worn methods of condemning everything on one side and praising everything on the other side of the political fence.

The day has gone by when you can fool people into believing that the nation, or a state or a county or a city is going to the dogs just because one political party happens to be in power in it. People are sick of the kind of editorial writing which sees only good in every measure and every man sponsored by one party and only bad on the other side. So, too, it is the little provincial papers that today in the news-columns magnify as first page news any disagreement in their opponents' camps and run only a half inch on the back page about any trouble in their own camp.

That is one reason why the bitterly partisan press is losing its influence in this country. The other reason is that there is more and better education everywhere and readers do not as much as formerly take the views and news of a one-sided paper as Gospel Truth. I told Mr. Hayden I hoped he would get some Republican to write each week in this paper, but if he can't find one, I shall try to be as fair as I can.

Take as an example this visit of Senator Heflin to make a speech in Dutchess County. The Senator had a legal right to speak and probably the large majority of his audience went to hear him out of sheer curiosity. Probably no man in the United States has done more to help the nomination of, and increase the support for Governor Smith all over this country than Senator Heflin.

He has made the nation realize that old fashioned bigotry does exist, a little of it in every section and a lot of it in some places and that the time has come to prove definitely that it must not and cannot be a controlling factor in our national life.

Here is a story about the Ku Klux Klan that could almost be called a Parable—but it is a true story and happened to me.

Three years ago I was the guest of honor at a Chamber of Commerce Banquet in a small city in Georgia. It was a community of almost pure Scotch and English Protestant ancestry. I sat on the right of the Mayor of the Town and on the other side of me sat the Secretary of the Chamber of Commerce, a young man born in Italy, and a Roman Catholic. Just beyond sat a Jew who was a member of the Executive Committee.

I turned to the Mayor and asked him if the Ku Klux Klan was strong in the city. He said "Yes, very." (It has since then nearly died out.) Then I asked if most of the members of the Chamber belonged to the Klan, and again he said "Yes."

Then I said, "If that is so, why is it that the Secretary is a Catholic and that a Jew is on the Executive Committee?"

He turned to me utterly surprised and answered: "Why, Mr. Roosevelt, we know those men. They are intimate friends of ours, we respect them and like them. You know this Klan business doesn't apply to people you know!"

I often wonder if those unfortunates who are working in open defiance of that article of the Constitution of the United States which guarantees religious liberty are also opposed to the great commandment, "Thou shalt love thy neighbor as thyself."

Think it over.

FRANKLIN D. ROOSEVELT

July 30, 1928

2

"I Am Hopeful Enough to Believe That Many Factors in Modern American Life Are Decreasing the Numbers of Misinformed or Unreasoning Voters"

Thursday, August 9, 1928

IT IS a little early in this campaign to discuss the platforms of the two major parties, for it is an undoubted fact that these platforms have to be considered in the light of what the candidates say about the issues in the acceptance and later speeches. So this is not yet the time for voters who are not bound by a party collar to make up their minds as to their final decision on November 6th.

Meanwhile it is the season of the whisperers who have a ready audience in hot weather, and it is an unfortunate fact that plenty of otherwise sane people listen eagerly to wild inventions about the personalities of candidates. No man in public life is free from this underhand attack, nor their families.

Grover Cleveland was accused of heavy drinking; so was Theodore Roosevelt; and every campaign starts a new series of wild stories. Yesterday's mail brings me four letters, two of them making wholly untrue insinuations about Secretary Hoover's personal habits, the other two about Governor Smith's. As I happen to be a personal friend of both of these gentlemen it makes me a little hot under the collar, because it hardly seems a fair reward to these two men who have given so many years of their lives to unselfiish public service.

That sort of letter, because it is signed and written in apparent good faith, has of course to be answered. But there is another variety, the unsigned letter, and these come every day in literally enormous numbers. They are silly letters, foul, dirty letters, threatening letters—and of course they go promptly to the fire. The pity of it is that there are still so many gullible or unthinking people in our midst.

I say "still," because I am hopeful enough to believe that many factors in modern American life are decreasing the numbers of misinformed or unreasoning voters. First of all, our educational system is improving everywhere, and most men and women read far more newspapers and magazines than in the last generation.

Then, too, our friends and neighbors cover a much wider geographical field than formerly. Better transportation, especially through the automobile and good roads, has enlarged the acquaintance and, with that, the point of view of everybody. I am inclined to think, with a recent visiting foreigner, that Henry Ford by providing the first cheap car did more than any other man of this generation to introduce Americans to themselves and end sectionalism and local narrowness. It is, for instance, hard to realize that it is only 18 years since Dick Connell and I made the first complete automobile campaign through this congressional district—someone else tried it in 1906 and scared so many horses that he had to quit!

As the years go by this new habit of travel is going to do much for the nation, not only industrially and socially, but in the political aspect also. We shall break down the barriers of distance, and find, for example, that we people in the east are very much the same type of Americans in thought, in life, and inspirations as our compatriots in Kansas or Oregon or Alabama.

So, too, the day will come when both political parties will be strong in every state of the nation. The two party system seems best suited for our governing needs, and gives a responsibility which would be hard to place if we had a large number of parties or "blocs." But this two party system ought to exist everywhere.

Let me say frankly that it would be a good thing for the south if they had a strong Republican party, but as at present constituted it can make no permanent headway there. Equally is it true that in places like Maine and Vermont and parts of upstate New York progress is hindered by an almost unanimous Republican vote.

The finest people in the world, whether in business or in public life, fail after a time to give their best efforts to serve if they know that they have a life job or have the power to choose their successors. ·

Probably it was this thought that caused the framers of

the Constitution to decide on a four year President instead of a King, and to give Senators a six year term instead of life tenure.

— If political leaders come to understand that the control of the government will be turned over to the other party when there is lack of vision and honesty and efficiency, we shall have better government at Washington.

FRANKLIN D. ROOSEVELT

Hyde Park, Aug. 5, 1928

3

"People Who See in a National Political Campaign Only One Conceivable Issue"

Thursday, August 16, 1928

MY MAIL each day brings me a dozen or more letters from Republicans and Democrats who seem to have merry-go-round minds. They start at a given point, follow a circular track, move with great rapidity and keep on coming back time after time to the same point. They are the people who see in a national political campaign only one conceivable issue. Some of them can think of nothing but agriculture, others of the tariff, others of foreign affairs, still others of the Volstead law.

Most of these letters contribute very little to the argument one way or the other, because it is obvious that the writers, having only one principal thought in life, are unable to view even that pet hobby with a broad and unprejudiced outlook. Every once in a while, however, I get a pretty good theme out of these merry-go-round letters. For instance, one old lady writes, "It would be a fine thing if we could stop worrying about the return of the public saloon. That is gone forever. It is time to start a campaign against the private saloon—I mean those that are situated between the chin and the nose of millions of Americans, and are running wide open." Democrats and Republicans alike who want to further the cause of a temperate nation can subscribe to that!

It is very easy for partisan political writers to tell you that this and that campaign of the past was decided on this or that issue, though there may have been, of course, one issue which stood out more prominently than the others. For instance, Free Silver was by no means the only determining factor in 1896. Thousands of old-line Democrats who did not believe in Bryan's 16-1 theory voted for him, and thousands of Free Silver Republicans maintained their party regularity by voting for McKinley. In 1916 Wilson was re-elected not because "He kept us out of war," but because of a fairly general satisfaction with the constructive and administrative results of his first administration. In 1920, the huge majority of President Harding's was not gained just on the League of Nations' issue—thousands voted for him in the honest belief that he would find some practical method by which we could join the league.

It is another curious fact that in most national campaigns the issue which seems to be prominent in July and August often becomes of minor importance in September and October.

During the past month it is true that the Volstead Law Amendment question has seemed to be the most prominent issue of the present campaign. Perhaps the wish is father to the thought, but I am frankly hopeful that by the time another month rolls round this particular matter will have been relegated to its proper place among all the other issues and that there will be a more and more widespread discussion of, and interest in, all the other differences between the two major parties.

After all, the success or failure of the next national administration will not be judged in history merely by the action of Congress on the Volstead Law. In the last analysis the individual voter ought to make up his final decision on the way he answers three big questions:

1. Am I satisfied with the conduct of the national government by the Republican party during the past four years or do I believe that it is best for the country that it be given a chance to take a 4-year vacation because of its record?

2. Looking at the dozen or more fairly broad questions of future policy as outlined in the platforms and speeches, which party offers the most good to the nation if put in power?

3. Looking at the candidates, their records as public servants and the campaigns they are making, which one is the best fitted to conduct the executive office of President during the next four years?

FRANKLIN D. ROOSEVELT

Hyde Park, August 11th, 1928

4

"Why in the Name of Common Sense Can't Civic Matters Be Eliminated from Partisan Politic?"

Thursday, August 23, 1928

BEFORE taking up more about political issues of the national campaign, I want to discuss very briefly a subject which ought not to be political, but is too frequently. I refer to the development of parks, parkways and outdoor facilities for the benefit of the many by the national, state and local government. A couple of hundreds of years ago all land was owned by a very small class in the community, and even 50 years ago any effort to provide outdoor, public recreation areas for the masses of the people would have been called rank socialism.

With our own generation, America has discovered the big outdoors. The rise of athletics, the advent of the automobile, and the better understanding of hygiene, have brought the city dwellers into contact with the wide open spaces. We of the country districts have had many a laugh over the ignorance of the city bred who are flocking into our midst. Last month a bus load of boys from the East Side of New York was being taken over a dirt road to a Dutchess County camp. As one of them saw a cow in the field, he exclaimed: "Gee, what kind of an animal is that?" It was his first cow. A little farther on a big rabbit ran along the road, and the boys on the front seat cried, "My, what is that? Is it a baby kangaroo?"

Hundreds of thousands of farm families are leaving the occupation of agriculture and moving to the cities; at the same time, hundreds of thousands of city dwellers are seeking the country districts for holidays, for sport, for recreation and for health. Obviously, private philanthropy is not going to provide camping areas and recreational facilities for the city dwellers, and the owners of farms and other private property are not welcoming the influx of people who don't know a rabbit from a kangaroo. It, therefore, seems clear that if we recognize the value to the human race of the trend to the outdoor life we must, through governmental machinery, provide adequate facilities. That is the system which underlies the great park programs of the various governmental agencies, especially our own State of New York.

Down in Long Island, a bitter fight has been raging between a handful of private property owners and the State Park Commission over the extension of two great parkways, conceived with the purpose of giving access to beaches, woods, and fresh air for the benefit of the 7,000,000 inhabitants of greater New York. Most of us can recognize the disturbed feelings of the owners of costly estates who are horrified at the invasion of their privacy by the multitudes who will use a new parkway cutting directly through their lands, but in the final analysis there seems to be no question that the fight will be won by the multitudes, because more and more we are, as a nation, working for the greatest good of the greatest number.

It is all very well to talk of the sanctity of private property, yet since the earliest days our institutions have recognized the right of eminent domain "on behalf of citizens where the taking of privately owned property will benefit the body of citizens." These growing needs are now being recognized by planning for the days to come. For instance, the Taconic State Park Commission, of which I happen to be a member, has jurisdiction over planning of this nature in the counties of Putnam, Dutchess, Columbia and Rensselaer. We are basing our plans on the assumption of a constantly growing population into these Hudson River counties, and a recognition of the obvious fact that if the State can acquire the needed lands for parks and parkways, the cost to the taxpayers will be only a fraction of what it would be 25 years from now. Westchester County is spending between fifty and sixty million dollars for lands which it now has to acquire at very high prices.

Every community in Dutchess County will show extraordinary growth in these coming years. I wish much that we might have a County Planning Commission. It would save vast sums by the prevention of costly mistakes, and encourage the use and enjoyment of several hundred thousand acres which are now unused or inaccessible. The chief drawback in the minds of most thinking citizens is that planning and park commissions of this kind would probably become political in their makeup. If the movement were started by a Board of Supervisors or by a Town Board or by a City Council, the chances are that the whole effort would take on a political color. More jobs. More money to spend. More publicity for somebody.

Why in the name of common sense can't civic matters of this kind be eliminated from partisan politics?

FRANKLIN D. ROOSEVELT

Hyde Park, August 18, 1928

5

"The Country Has Little to Fear From Any Drastic Tariff Changes by Either Republicans or Democrats"

Thursday, August 30, 1928

IF OTHER people are like me, they are likely to lay aside the morning paper which contains a party platform, or a speech of acceptance, with every good intention in the world of reading it later, but the good intention generally gets no further. That is why, for the next few weeks, I shall quote from the platforms and from the speeches of acceptance.

In these short informal talks it is going to be a difficult task to discuss more than the broad generalities of the issue, but I shall try to be fair and give the principal arguments on both sides.

We might just as well leave out entirely the opening paragraphs of both Republican and Democratic platforms. The Republicans claim that every good thing that has happened anywhere during the past eight years has been due to Republican wisdom; the Democrats insist that if we are to have prosperity and happiness during the next four years we must put them in power.

Today I should like to dispose of one issue which will not bulk as large in the campaign this year as it did 30 or 40 years ago—the tariff.

The Republican platform reaffirms, of course, its support of a protective tariff, and then goes on with these interesting words:

"While certain provisions of the present law require revision, in the light of changes in the world competitive situation since its enactment, the record of the country since 1922 clearly shows that the fundamental protective principle of the law has been fully justified."

"However we realize that there are certain industries which cannot successfully compete with foreign producers because of lower foreign wages and a lower cost of living abroad, and we pledge the next Republican Congress to an examination, and, where necessary, a revision of tariff schedules . . ."

The Democratic tariff plank reads:

"The Democratic tariff legislation will be based on the following policies:

1. Maintenance of legitimate business and a high standard of wages for American labor. 2. Increasing the purchasing power of wages and income by reduction of monopolistic and extortionist tariff rates. 3. Restoration of the Wilson conception of a fact-finding tariff commission. 4. Duties that will permit effective competitions, insure against monopoly, and produce a fair revenue for the support of the government.

5. Safeguarding the public against monopoly created by special tariff favors. 6. Equitable distribution of the benefits and burdens of the tariff among all."

Mr. Hoover, in his acceptance speech, says:

"We have pledged ourselves to make such provisions in the tariff laws as may be necessary to provide real protection against the shiftings of economic tide in various industries."

Governor Smith says:

"The Democratic Party does not, and under my leadership will not, advocate any sudden or drastic revolution in our economic system which would cause business upheaval and popular distress. . . .

"In an administration anxious to meet political obligations, the tariff commission has ceased to function . . . I shall restore this commission . . . in order that, properly manned, it may produce the facts that will enable us to ascertain how we may increase the purchasing power of everybody's income or wages by the adjustment of those schedules which are now the result of log-rolling and which, upon their face, are extortionate and unnecessary."

When all is said and done, the tariff question is not going to be one of the great issues of this campaign. Put into the simplest language here are the positions of the two parties:

The Republicans say that the present tariff has worked well and we shall adjust it in the future to meet changing needs.

The Democrats say, first, what is wrong with the present tariff is that it is the result of log-rolling and unduly favors certain pet industries, and does not take care of others, secondly, favoritism in the tariff laws should be eliminated by taking the tariff out of politics and putting the principle of adequate protection on a fact-finding basis by restoring the scientific fact-finding activities of a non-partisan tariff commission.

I suppose that a number of antiquated orators and editorial writers will still seek to tell the credulous that if the Democrats win they will put in free trade and close up all our factories. The fact remains that one of the really significant events of the past month has been the number of important business and industrial leaders who have announced that they will vote the Democratic ticket.

In other words, in the last analysis, the country has little to fear from any drastic tariff changes by either Republicans or Democrats. The Republicans, if returned to power, will make few changes of any importance. The Democrats, if successful, will try to take the tariff out of politics and stop what they call favoritism.

Take your choice.

FRANKLIN D. ROOSEVELT

Hyde Park, August 25, 1928

6

"The Seriousness of the Agricultural Situation in the United States"

Thursday, September 6, 1928

THE PROBLEM of relief for agriculture may not seem to people living in the eastern states to be one which amounts to much. It may be perfectly true that half the population of the country lives in cities but it is also true that the other half of all our citizens are still more or less directly connected with the pursuit of raising crops of one kind or another for a livelihood.

As proving the seriousness of the agricultural situation in the United States at the present time, both the Republican and Democratic platforms this year devote more space to this topic than to any other. For that reason and because it is a real campaign issue this year I shall have to discuss it in at least two of these weekly articles and do a certain amount of quotation.

Before giving the platforms and the candidates' statements, I want first to give a few significant figures. We know for instance, that the wheat growers of the United States are getting about $1.10 a bushel, and it is clearly established that the cost of raising each bushel is about $1.20. Figures show that in the corn belt there are an average of 444 farm failures every working day and an average of 3½ bank failures every working day. There is an average mortgage or crop indebtedness of $35 per acre on these farms, and 86 per cent of all this farming land is mortgaged.

Coming closer home we know what the farmers are getting for their potatoes and their milk in Dutchess County; and I could go on indefinitely to illustrate the simple fact that the great mass of the farmers of America are getting less than any peasant laborer in any European country in return for their work.

I am not stating these facts as a partisan but I am merely bringing out what a whole lot of politicians would like to have covered up.

It may be true that from the industrial point of view the United States has been on the whole prosperous during the past years, but it is unsound and untrue to talk about general prosperity when every day that passes a thousand families are being driven out of their homes by the farm economic collapse for which no governmental remedy has been found.

It is not as if this situation were a development of the past year or two. It has been going on steadily and becoming increasingly serious to our national welfare ever since the close of the World War.

If it be true that the nation cannot endure half slave and half free, so it is equally true that a nation cannot endure with industrial prosperity and agricultural ruin.

Men in public life in Washington, in the administration and in Congress, have been trying to find some remedy by which the very existence of the agricultural class of America could be saved and put back on its feet. Every state has joined in the plea just as every section in the country fifteen years ago was calling for the establishment of a sound national banking system. The demand for the solution of the banking problem met an answer in the splendid Federal Reserve Act of the first Wilson Administration, but eight years of pleas from the farmers of the east, west and south have met with no relief.

To go into the reasons for such hopeless failure on the part of the national government would be a waste of time, but it stands out as a sad fact.

It is, however, fair and necessary to recall the fact that twice recently, laws have been passed and later vetoed by President Coolidge. These laws undertook to solve the most difficult problems of the national agricultural crops [sic] which were to market the surplus crops, or in other words the excess over normal home consumption. The principal objection of President Coolidge in vetoing the agricultural bills was to the plan devised for taking care of these surpluses and distributing the loss involved in selling these surpluses abroad among all the growers of the crop.

It seems to be the perfectly obvious fact that some means must be found for taking care of these surpluses; yet on this very point hangs the differences between the two great parties.

In other words the Republican platform follows the vetoes of President Coolidge in fearing to undertake the solution of the problem of the surpluses. On the other hand the Democratic Platform distinctly undertakes to deal with crop surpluses.

It would take two columns to give the agricultural planks of the platforms as a whole and I shall try to boil them down without bias.

The Republican plank says: "We promise every assistance to the reorganization of the marketing system on sounder and more economic lines . . . the Republican party pledges itself to the enactment of legislation creating a Federal Farm Board cloaked with the necessary powers to establish a farm marketing system, of farmer-owned and farmer-controlled surpluses through orderly distribution. We favor adequate tariff protection to such of our agricultural products as are affected by foreign competition. We favor, without putting the Government into business, the establishment of a Federal system for cooperative and orderly marketing of farm products."

The Democratic platform, which evidently was satisfactory to the leaders of the principal farm organizations, starts off by calling attention to the complete failure of the Republican party to give relief to agricultural distress during the past eight years and to the evident discrimination in favor of industry and against agriculture. It then says, "We pledge the united efforts of the legislative and executive branches of government . . . to the immediate enactment of such legislation and to other steps as are necessary to place and maintain the purchasing power of farm products and the complete economic equality of agriculture . . . we pledge that in its tariff the Democratic party will insist on equality of treatment between agriculture and other industries . . . to give this equality a remedy must be found which will include among other things;

a. Credit aid by loans to cooperatives on at least as favorable a basis as the government aid to the Merchant Marine.

b. Creation of Federal Farm Board to assist . . . in the marketing of products as the Federal Reserve Board has done for the bankers and business men.

c. Reduction through proper governmental agencies of the spread between what the farmer gets and what the ultimate consumer pays, with consequent benefit to both.

d. Consideration of the condition of agriculture in the formulation of government financial and tax measures.

"We pledge the party to foster and develop cooperative marketing associations through appropriate governmental aid.

"We recognize that experience has demonstrated that members of such associations alone cannot successfully assume the full responsibility for a program that benefits all producers alike. We pledge the party to an earnest endeavor to solve this problem of the distribution of the cost of dealing with crop surpluses over the marketed units of the crops whose producers are benefitted by such assistance."

There is one important and vital difference between the two parties. The Republicans would help the farmer of the nation to expand the cooperative principle (in other words, as some have said, to find the way out of their own difficulties).

The Democratic platform on the other hand, taking the parallel of the Federal Reserve Act, proposes a Federal Farm system which without subsidies but with Federal leadership, protection and organization will help the farmer to solve national matters like crop surpluses where the local cooperation is obviously not in a position to get results. There is a mighty difference between the two programs.

Next week I shall point out some further differences that have become apparent since the acceptance speeches of Secretary Hoover and Governor Smith.

Franklin D. Roosevelt

Hyde Park, Sept. 1, 1928

7

"This Question of the Influence of the Tariff on Agriculture"

Thursday, September 13, 1928

LAST WEEK in discussing agriculture I tried to summarize the two platform planks. The acceptance speeches of the candidates bring out some other points.

Mr. Hoover says, "We have pledged ourselves to find a solution . . . an adequate tariff is the foundation of farm relief. I would use my office to influence the giving to the farmers the full benefit of our historic tariff policy . . . The modernization of our great system of inland waterways will comprise a most substantial method of farm relief . . . The outstanding proposal of party program is the pledge to undertake the reorganization of the marketing system upon sounder and more economical lines." He then reiterates the platform suggestion to build up farmers' cooperative and farmer-owned stabilizing corporations.

Governor Smith says, "The tariff is ineffective on commodities on which there is exportable surplus. Our platform points the way to making a tariff effective for crops for which we produce a surplus. If the government interferes with one phase of economic life by the tariff, by assistance to the Merchant Marine, by control of the flow of money and capital through the banking system, it is bad logic, bad economics to abandon our governmental responsibility and say that as to agriculture alone, the Government should not aid. Cooperative control of markets and warehouses for surplus farm products is essential just as cooperative control of the flow of capital was found necessary . . . If I am elected I shall immediately after election ask leaders of the type I have named, irrespective of party, to enter upon this task. I shall join them in the discharge of their duties during the coming winter and present to Congress, upon its convening, the solution recommended by the body of men best fitted to render this signal service to the nation. I shall supervise the activities of this body until satisfactory law is placed upon the Statute Books."

Why Mr. Hoover has dragged in a higher tariff as one of the remedies for a sick agricultural situation, I am not quite clear. Strictly agricultural imports into the United States are negligible and I see no reason why the tariff should not be adjusted from time to time so as to prevent foreign competition with all of our leading crops. A scientifically adjustable tariff such as is proposed by the Democratic platform would take care of a changing condition from year to year and eliminate any possibility of cheaply raised foreign crops from competing with our home grown crops.

This reminds me of some of the nonsense which always finds its way into campaigns. Even so-called statesmen are not above using it if they think they can get away with it. For instance, last week in a New England city my friend Senator Curtis, the Republican nominee for Vice-President, told his city audience with due solemnity that last year we imported three billion dollars' worth of agricultural products. He could not have tried to make the implication that foreign farmers are competing with our farmers and that the higher tariff would solve the difficulty if he had been talking to an audience of farmers in his own state of Kansas but he thought he could fool a city audience in the East. He forgot to mention the fact that the so-called agricultural imports into the United States are made up almost wholly of things that we cannot raise in this country. For instance, we import vast quantities of rubber and sisal and bananas and in fact all of the products of the tropics.

When we come down to this question of the influence of the tariff on agriculture, I have never yet found any expert on the tariff in either party who would not admit in the final analysis that the farmer sells his goods in a world-wide and therefore unprotected market and buys the machinery for his farm and the clothes for his family in a highly protected national market.

The only bearing that the tariff has on the farmers is, first, that the tariff ought to prevent him from having to compete with imports of fruit, grain, potatoes, and other crops we can raise here and at the same time it ought to prevent him from being gouged by especially favored monopolies when he buys the necessary farm supplies.

The real meat in the cocoanut in this election lies in two issues that are becoming more clearly drawn every day.

First the Republican party makes various pledges as to what it will do but it is unable to escape the knowledge on the part of every farmer that it has failed for eight years to give him any substantial relief.

In other words a reliance on the Republican promises for the future must overlook the complete failure to carry out the pledges of the party made in 1920 and 1924. The Democratic party naturally has no recent record on which to come before the people, for it has been out of power both in the White House and in Congress. However, its record of solving the banking and currency situation through the definite adoption of a very practical Federal Reserve Act immediately after it came into power in 1913 leads many to believe that there is more probability of achieving definite and immediate results with a new broom.

As to the candidates themselves Mr. Hoover's proposal is based obviously on the desire not to repudiate the vetoes of President Coolidge of the markets feature of relief [sic] rather than to the tackling of the problem of the crop surplus.

Governor Smith on the other hand while recognizing the full value of cooperative markets sees at the same time the tremendous problem of the crop surpluses, and pledges that immediately after election he will if successful work out the method for accomplishing their control, aided by the best expert advice, and that he will make legislation to attain the end desired the immediate object of his government.

As the campaign goes on there will probably be much talk and no little confusion of the complex problems of agriculture and it is of the utmost importance that the voting public should try to resolve the issues down to their simplest form.

Many voters will still trust to Mr. Hoover and a Republican Congress to get some form of relief for our farmers. If the Republicans are successful, I sincerely hope that their trust will not have been misplaced.

Many other voters of both parties will feel that the failure of the Harding and Coolidge administrations to accomplish anything for the relief of the farmers entitles them to transfer their confidence to Governor Smith and the Democratic party, keeping in mind also the thought that Governor Smith has shown extraordinary ability to work successfully with the legislative branch of the Government and to achieve practical and definite results.

Franklin D. Roosevelt

Hyde Park, Sept. 8th, 1928.

8

"The Important Thing Is Not to Resolve Against War, But to Eliminate the Causes of War Before Those Causes Get to a Serious Climax"

Thursday, September 20, 1928

S O FAR in this campaign the subject of our relations with other nations has been generally overlooked. It is, however, of vital interest to our lives and those of our children.

There are two ways of looking at this big and vital subject. First, we ought to be interested from the viewpoint of the good of humanity in general, in the elimination of disagreements and quarrels and war because, after all, this is only an extension to the larger field of what right-minded people are trying to do with their own lives in their own communities.

Secondly, honest friendship between different nations means much from the practical point of view of prosperity because if we are disliked or have serious points of differences with foreign nations our commercial trade backwards and forwards is necessarily injured.

The broad difference between the platforms of the two parties this year is this: The Republicans point with pride to the foreign policy of the past eight years and especially to the multilateral treaties renouncing war which are now being signed by various nations; the Democratic platform, on the other hand, while endorsing the renouncing of war, calls attention to the dislike in which this nation is held by most of the other nations of the world and specifically opposes the kind of unofficial interference in the affairs of our neighbors of which our [sic] Nicaragua is an example. Further, the Democratic platform condemns the Republican administration for its failure to expand the work for the limitation of armaments and its failure to prevent the continuation of competitive building of naval ships at an increasingly costly rate.

In the acceptance speeches of Secretary Hoover and of Governor Smith, both definitely oppose any entangling alliances. Secretary Hoover again stands on the accomplishments of the Coolidge administration and Governor Smith comes out strongly against interference in the purely internal affairs of our Latin American neighbors.

I should like to bring out one or two points which will probably become clearer as the campaign progresses. It seems to me that Democrats and Republicans alike can give credit to Secretary Kellogg for the multilateral treaties renouncing war which are now being signed by many nations. These treaties constitute an excellent expression of good will and future policy. It is a fine thing to resolve against using war as an instrument of settling international disputes but there are two distinctly weak points in the accomplishment. The first is the fact that defensive war is specifically excepted from these treaties and nobody has ever yet been able to get nations to define what they mean by defensive war.

It is, however, worth while to recall that not very long ago Germany and Austria were proclaiming to the world that the invasion of Belgium and France in 1914 was a wholly defensive act. In other words, this very practical question of who is the aggressor has not in any way been solved by Mr. Kellogg's treaties.

Furthermore we must remember, as practical people, that for several thousand years nations have in many instances entered into solemn treaties of permanent peace and friendship. That word "permanent" was in effect a pious resolution of the moment that they would never go to war with each other again; but unfortunately history records that these pious resolutions were duly forgotten or explained away when these same nations got involved in some subsequent quarrel.

The real meat of it is that while we can be proud of our present declarations, we must be practical enough to realize that they do not go to the root of the trouble. The important thing is not to resolve against war, but to eliminate the causes of war before those causes get to a serious climax.

Our own future foreign policy, to be sure, must not involve us in any entangling alliances but at the same time we ought to begin right away to do a great deal more than we are doing now to cooperate with other nations in the practical working out of more methods for settling international disputes in their earlier stages. Today we are very much aloof in this work.

We are apt to forget that other nations are doing effective work each year in settling all manner of world wide problems and that our part in this work has been wholly negligible. We have lost our leadership of the moral forces of mankind and have contributed nothing officially to the settlement of international problems.

Frankly, I was a little amused the other day when my friend, Mr. Hoover, tried to take credit for two alleged accomplishments of past few years. First he talked about the naval disarmament treaty of 1921. This was a fine treaty in that it postponed the building of ships over 10,000 tons until 1931. But the result hoped for has not proved so good. Naval nations stopped building battle ships but they immediately started into a race to build cruisers under 10,000 tons. The result is that this past year the Coolidge administration asked for $75,000,000 to build new naval ships—a far larger amount than had ever been asked for before except during the late war.

Secondly, Mr. Hoover talked about the Dawes Commission which so successfully put through the plan to finance the reparations in Europe. This amused me more than a little because it is a matter of record that President Coolidge declined officially to have anything to do with the Commission. Messrs. Dawes, Young and Robinson went to Europe as private citizens on the invitation of the Reparations Commission and Mr. Coolidge made it clear to the United States that his administration had nothing to do with them. A few months later these three gentlemen came back with their task accomplished. Then our President patted them on the back and tried to make people believe that they had some connection with our own State Department.

The really serious fact today is that this country is not liked by its neighbors. No one who has studied the situation at first hand can deny this. If the attitude of other nations toward us could be put on a more friendly basis it would do much to help our own prosperity back home. Hundreds of exporters of American products will tell you that they are handicapped in selling American goods abroad by the fact that foreigners dislike us so much that they would rather buy from other nations.

South and Central America furnish excellent examples of this. We are viewed with suspicion throughout Latin America because of our general attitude in the past. Governor Smith proposes a definite American policy of non-interference in the internal affairs of our Latin American neighbors.

Much can be done in these next few years both in the cause of peace and also in the cause of regaining friendships which have been lost. In the last analysis our foreign relations ought not to be a strictly partisan question. We need the laying down of a policy which will be satisfactory to Americans of all parties—a policy which will help our prosperity and at the same time promote the cause of peace through the elimination of the causes of trouble, and promote our own prosperity by making people understand that we are not working for purely selfish ends.

FRANKLIN D. ROOSEVELT

Hyde Park,
Dutchess County, N. Y.
For the "Standard," September 15, 1928

9

"The Problem of Water Power Sites"

Thursday, September 27, 1928

THERE is one subject on which there is a fairly clear divergence of principle between the two candidates and to a certain extent between the two parties—the general problem of water power sites.

It is impossible in a short article to explain just where state authority over water power ends and Federal authority begins, but it is worth while to restate in plain language the principles involved whether they may be of state or national interest.

The general use of electricity continues to grow by leaps and bounds and it is probably safe to assert that unless some new form of power is discovered we as a nation soon will require for all sorts of uses all of the electric current that is capable of being generated by all of the rivers and streams of the United States.

Here are the two schools of thought in regard to the development of hydro-electric power, whether the stream be under the control of the state or of the Federal Government.

As a general proposition the Republican party believes that the governmental authorities should issue practically perpetual charters or franchises to private corporations and that these private corporations should develop the power sites and distribute the electric current to the homes, farms and industries of given territories. The Republicans would require some form of rental for the use of the water and while they would give these franchises ostensibly for definite periods of time such as sixty or ninety years, it is of course obvious that the franchises, issued for such a party [sic] holds that to do other than this is to put the government in some way into business and they talk a great deal about the dangers of government ownership and operation. It is their theory that by setting up Public Service Commissions the rate charged by the private companies to the consumer can be kept down to a fair level.

Governor Smith in this state and other Democrats in other states have offered a different plan. They are opposed to letting the government lose physical control of the actual power site and they propose that the government itself, through a government owned corporation or "authority" should do the actual construction of the necessary dams and power houses and should install the electrical generating machinery therein. They would then sell the current thus produced to privately owned electric power and light corporations for distribution to the consumer. They point out that this course does not really put the government into business, that the necessary dams and power houses can be built and equipped just as efficiently by the government as by private capital and that the real cost of producing the power is made actually very much cheaper because the government can raise the necessary money on a 4 per cent basis or lower, whereas private companies can only raise money by paying 8 per cent or more.

Further, the Democratic theory points out that the operation of a power plant requires very few employes and that the actual production of power by the government can be done just as cheaply and efficiently year in and year out as by a private company. Under this plan the distribution of power over the transmission lines and into the homes and factories, the maintenance and repairs, the reading of meters, collecting of bills and all the other factors which require a large staff of employees would continue to be done by privately operated companies as it is today.

It seems to me important that people in this country should not be carried away by mere words. We often hear it said that Government operation of anything under the sun is socialistic. If that is so our postal service is socialistic, so is the parcel post which has largely taken place of the old express companies; so are the public highways which took the place of toll roads. In other words, the American people are willing to let the government engage in business of certain kinds where it can do so better than private companies. It is felt by many that on this water power matter the government could well develop the water power sites itself, not only saving money in that development, but also retaining physical control over the sites and selling the electrical current to private companies for distribution.

This would seem to be the Democratic program for the development of some of the Federally owned water power sites such as Muscle Shoals and Boulder Dam. There may be a good deal in the thought that if the government retains control of these and other great sites, it will do much towards keeping a check on the prices for electrical current paid by the consumer. Electricity is of such vital and growing concern to every one of us in our daily lives that we have a right to demand that no individual or set of individuals should ever get into a position where they can make vast fortunes at our expense, especially by obtaining the primary sources of their power from rivers and streams that are owned by the citizens themselves.

In this great question every citizen in every state has a definite personal interest. Most of us are agreed that it would be a mistake under present conditions for the Washington Government or the state government to go into the whole business of distributing electrical power to all of us. But it is worth while for us to give serious attention to the desirability of allowing the several governments to own and control the actual power sites, letting private companies do the distribution.

In the final analysis the same difference between two schools of thought applies to the problem of the development of our natural resources. These resources both above and below ground are the common heritage of the people of the United States. They need to be developed and at the same time we must prevent them from being wasted. Many of the resources, such as our timber supply, are being exhausted. It is certainly a very necessary part of the function of our government to see that the use of these resources shall be allowed only for the best interests of the population as a whole and that no private individuals should be allowed to make huge profits at the expense of the great mass of ultimate consumers.

Mr. Hoover has, at this writing, said nothing definite about the development of the great power project now almost completed at Muscle Shoals. Governor Smith says "It will be the policy of my administration, while retaining governmental control, to develop a method of operation for Muscle Shoals which will reclaim for the government some fair revenue from the enormous expenditure already made for its development and which is now a complete waste. In this way the original peace time purpose of the construction of this plant will be achieved. The nation will be reimbursed, agriculture will be benefited by the cheap production of nitrates for fertilizer and the surplus power will be distributed to the people."

FRANKLIN D. ROOSEVELT

Hyde Park, Dutchess County, New York.
For the "Standard," September 22, 1928

IO

"One Subject in This Campaign Happens to be an Old Pet of Mine . . . For Many Years in Washington I Harped on the Extravagance and Inefficiency of the Federal Governmental Structure"

Thursday, October 4, 1928

ONE subject in this campaign happens to be an old pet of mine. For many years when I was in Washington I harped on the extravagance and inefficiency of the Federal governmental structure—dozens of wholly uncoordinated departments, commissions, bureaus, agencies, etc., etc., duplicating each other in work, stepping on each other's toes and causing general confusion. I am very glad to see that this subject has come to the front again.

Back in 1920 this was one of the campaign issues raised by

Mr. Harding and he promised to accomplish great things if he was returned to power. Soon after his inauguration a plan was worked out with the help of his cabinet which, of course, included Mr. Hoover. This plan was widely heralded as a consolidation of these dozens of departments and bureaus, the elimination of unnecessary ones and general placing of the governmental machinery in Washington on a business basis. Some times it is a very unfortunate thing to have a long memory because it makes one think of disagreeable failures that took place many years ago. It is a sad but true fact that this grand little plan of 1921 seems to have completely disappeared from view in the succeeding seven years. It is unfortunate but true that there are just exactly as many bureaus and departments and commissions and agencies in existence today in Washington as there were then and nobody in their wildest dreams can claim that anything substantial has been accomplished in pursuance of that solemn promise made eight years ago by Mr. Harding.

Now, the point of this particular article is to point out, in all fairness, that Mr. Hoover has said in his speech of acceptance that he proposes to do a lot along the lines of consolidation and rearranging the Federal government if he is elected. He cites instances of scattering of functions and confusion of responsibility in the Federal organization. We have, for instance, 14 different bureaus engaged in public works and construction located in 9 different departments of the government. Now I for one have no doubt in my mind that Secretary Hoover is perfectly sincere in wanting to accomplish something practical towards the consolidation and improvement of the governmental machine.

However, in order to be fair it is necessary to point out that on the other side of the picture we have a record, not merely of promises, but of actual accomplishment. Governor Smith found in the Albany governmental machine a situation very similar to that at Washington. Realizing that in order to get cooperation from the legislature it would be necessary to sell the idea to the public, he started a campaign of public education. The result was such a wave of public opinion that, with the assistance of a commission of noted citizens such as former Governor Hughes, he was able to secure a constitutional amendment and legislation which consolidated more than one hundred offices, commissions and boards into eighteen well coordinated departments, each one responsible to the Governor.

Governor Smith proposes to do the same fine quality of work in Washington as he has already accomplished in Albany and it is right to show that, while both candidates may be seeking the same purposes, one of them has a definite record of accomplishment behind him and the other has not, even though that other has been in a responsible position in the cabinet for seven years.

Just one other point on this question of making Federal government more efficient. Almost anything that is done in Washington requires the approval of the Congress of the United States. It is logical that the voters should give careful weight to the relative ability of Secretary Hoover and Governor Smith to deal with the Congress. Whichever one becomes President will have to sell his plan to the legislative branch of the Government. This is not an easy task. Its successful accomplishment will depend very largely on the personality of whichever man is elected in November. One of these men has been the head of a government department for over seven years and the history of what he has or has not been able to accomplish in the way of reorganization and consolidation of the governmental machinery is a matter of record. The other candidate has faced the same problems in regard to the greatest of our state governments and his record of definite accomplishment with the aid of the people and of the legislature of the state of New York is also an open book. My great personal hope as a private citizen is that the next administration and the next Congress will not stop at making investigations and reports, but will pass legislation to put through a general far-reaching reorganization of the whole governmental machine. Naturally I have my own personal opinion as to which candidate is more likely to accomplish this very necessary objective.

FRANKLIN D. ROOSEVELT

Hyde Park, Dutchess County, New York,
For the "Standard," September 29, 1928

MARGINALIA

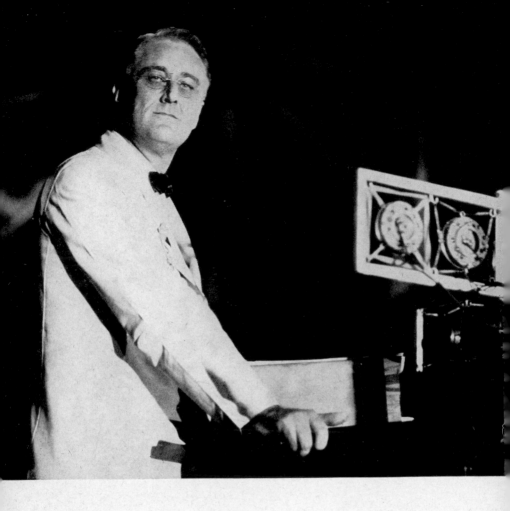

Mr. Roosevelt Nominating Alfred E. Smith

Houston, June, 1928

Marginalia

GENERAL

The Sources:

In the preparation of this volume, the editor used photostats of the original columns which appeared in the Macon *Daily Telegraph,* while the columns printed in the *Standard* were taken directly from the newspapers which the editor was able personally to examine. All are reprinted herein as they were originally published, except for corrections of typographical errors of the linotyper and the addition by the present writer of captions—usually a phrase or sentence taken from Mr. Roosevelt's text—giving some indication of the contents of each column. It was not possible to check all the columns as they appeared in print against a primary source such as a carbon copy of FDR's original typed manuscript. If sets of such copies have been preserved, they have not as yet found their way into his papers at the Franklin D. Roosevelt Library, Hyde Park, New York. They may be among the papers still in the hands of the executors of Mr. Roosevelt's estate.

In any case, it appears unlikely that a complete set of copies of the Macon column manuscripts will turn up. Tucked away in the volume of photostats referred to in the next note are carbon copies of the manuscripts of four of the columns and the first page of a fifth. These are accompanied by a memo on White House stationery headed "Memo for Mary" and signed "G" (Grace Tully, the President's secretary) stating that they are copies of FDR's 1925 columns and suggesting that a slip case be made for them. This leads one to believe that all the available copies are in this group, which is incomplete.

The editor has made use of the editorial tool *sic* to indicate missing words or garbled sentences in the original columns as printed. This was especially necessary in connection with the *Standard* columns where the quality of the printing was not always what it should be. Irregularities in capitalization and punctuation in the letters reprinted in the *Standard* have been left as found in the original printing. In no instance do the printing irregularities in either newspaper affect the sense of what has been printed.

FDR the President on FDR the Columnist:

In the President's Room of the Franklin D. Roosevelt Library are several locked bookcases. These contain what Mr. Roosevelt called his "A" books. These are books belonging to him which were not library property at the time of his death. According to Fred Shipman, director of the Library, Mr. Roosevelt was engaged in arranging on these shelves, books by and about himself and books by and about members of his family. One day in the summer of 1946 Mr. Shipman guided the editor through the throng milling about the library to view its exhibits and into the quiet of the President's Room. From one of the cases there was produced a pigskin bound volume of photostats of the *Telegraph* columns. The cover of the volume is stamped *Roosevelt Says*; and in the lower right hand corner it reads, *Being an Exegisis of the New Deal, April-May 1925.* This volume was prepared for Mr. Roosevelt and presented to him while he was President. On the flyleaf we learn what the President really thought of himself as a columnist; he has written:

> My first effort as a columnist—proving that no one can write a column on public affairs once a day, or twice a week.
> Franklin D. Roosevelt, 1937

"The Light of the Circumstances":

While it is the aim of this book to make these papers of Franklin Roosevelt available, rather than to appraise his opinions or his prose, readers might do well to keep in mind that which Eleanor Roosevelt wrote not long ago with regard to reading or quoting what a man has said at some earlier time:

> It has always seemed to me very unwise to quote people after they are dead. Their written documents, of course, can be considered in the light of the circumstances and the period in which they were written. They are factual and represent at least what the man himself put down at that period.
>
> Even that, I think, is sometimes misleading, because all intelligent people change their minds in view of changed circumstances and conditions. Only stupid people remain rigid and inflexible in their opinions and ideas. Therefore you can really never tell what a man who has been a thinker and a leader, in either public or private life, would think or do if he were alive and facing new circumstances. You can take what he has written and what he said and what you know of his character and principles, and it may influence you in your thinking. But it should never be considered as the attitude of the man in the new situation. A new decision should always be the result of new thinking.

The quotation is from *My Day,* syndicated newspaper column, October 25, 1945. Mrs. Roosevelt was writing regarding the quotation of an FDR letter to Ibn Saud stating the President's stand on the Arab-Jewish problem in Palestine.

The Roosevelt By-Line:

Of course, FDR wrote other contributions for newspapers. Typical were six articles written by Mr. Roosevelt as Assistant Secretary of the Navy on the condition of the U. S. Navy, which were syndicated by the Newspaper Enterprise Association. They appeared in the Cleveland *Press,* the Muskegon *Chronicle* and other newspapers during the period September 24, 1915 to October 15, 1915. On another occasion, as President of the Boy Scout Foundation of Greater New York, he wrote a feature article on the Boy Scouts of America, the New York *Times,* VIII, p. 18, August 12, 1928. These were semi-official writings which cannot be classified as the work of FDR as a newspaper columnist. For another example, see "Is There A Jefferson on the Horizon," a book review of Claude G. Bowers' *Jefferson and Hamilton: The Struggle for Democracy in America,* in the *Evening World* (New York), December 3, 1925, p. 21 (reprinted in *The American Mercury,* Vol. LXI, No. 261, p. 277, September 1945, with the editorial comment: "Viewed in retrospect it is a revealing document, for it seems to forecast many of the ideas and certainly a great deal of the mood of what later came to be known as the New Deal.").

The ex-Editor of the Crimson:

For Franklin Roosevelt's pride in his experience as editor of the Harvard *Crimson,* see Jonathan Daniels' "What I Learned About Washington", *The Saturday Evening Post,* Vol. 218, No. 39, March 30, 1946, p. 82, wherein a former Presidential administrative assistant to Mr. Roosevelt writes:

> I was not a bureaucrat . . . I hope I am still a reporter. I had had, with other newspapermen, to listen to enough politicians and officials say that they used to be newspapermen themselves. Franklin Roosevelt never quite got over having been an editor of the Harvard Crimson . . .

For other examples, see Milton MacKaye, "The Governor," *The New Yorker*, August 15th issue (reprinted in *The Roosevelt Omnibus*, edited and annotated by Don Wharton, New York: Alfred A. Knopf, 1934, p. 35); see also the present writer's interview with Mr. Roosevelt during the Presidential campaign of 1932, the Harvard *Crimson*, October 31, 1932, p. 1.

Mr. Roosevelt and the Working Press:

Throughout his long career as a public servant, beginning in 1910, FDR got on well with the people of the press. The late Raymond Clapper found this popularity due to several things: the personal relations between Mr. Roosevelt and the press were pleasant; he never sent reporters away empty-handed. Reporters admired his political craftsmanship; they believed his sincerity, his courage, his willingness to experiment; and they considered themselves among the common men for whom he pleaded and fought. Newspaper publishers did not always concur with their reporters on this subject ("Why Reporters Like Roosevelt," *Review of Reviews*, LXXXIX, p. 14, June 1934.). For another interesting comment on the relationship between Mr. Roosevelt and the Press, see L. C. Rosten, *The Washington Correspondents*, New York: Harcourt, Brace and Company, 1937, pp. 47-60. Especially interesting is Mr. Rosten's comment (p. 47) on FDR's press relations prior to his entering the Presidency; what is probably a minority view reads as follows:

> Mr. Roosevelt's earlier experiences with the press had not presaged such success. As Assistant Secretary of the Navy in the Wilson cabinet he had offended newspapermen, partly because of an "arrogant Harvard manner," in the words of one correspondent, partly because of several news hoaxes he played upon reporters covering the Navy Department. In his Vice-Presidential campaign of 1920,

Mr. Roosevelt had irritated the press by denying remarks which the newspapermen recalled his having made. When he was Governor of New York, friction between him and the press had broken out. At one point he "threatened" reporters for speculating on his disposition of charges against Mayor James J. Walker. In Albany, some reporters avoided his conferences altogether.

In 1937, FDR explained the attitude of reporters and publishers:

> ... I think it is generally conceded that the overwhelming number of newspapers in the United States, especially the larger papers, have been more or less critical of the New Deal policies in general and of my Administration in particular. This was true in the campaign of 1932, and even more true during the campaigns of 1934 and 1936— although all of these campaigns resulted in overwhelming popular endorsement of the aims, objectives and accomplishments of the New Deal.
>
> I consider it an interetsing fact that in spite of this array of editorial opposition, which apparently has been unable to exercise adequate influence upon public opinion in the United States, the great majority of newspaper correspondents who cover the White House are personally friendly to the Administration, and in general approve its objectives, most of its methods, and the legislation adopted to accomplish its goal. I know that a number of the newspaper correspondents who write so-called "unfriendly" articles are not personally opposed to the things they write about. I think that the first part of this anomaly can be explained by the fact that many hostile newspaper owners require their Washington correspondents to give their news dispatches a critical or unfriendly touch; and the second part, by the fact that correspondents themselves have such intimate contact with the day-by-day administration of affairs and with the views of those who make policy, that they have come to approve the objectives and not to share personally the oppositions displayed by their papers.
>
> In this I am referring only to the writers of what are

known as news stories. They are in a different class from columnists and writers of business news letters. In recent years the writings of these latter groups have found a ready market. In most cases their columns are based either on the pure imagination and invention of the writer or on untrue gossip which, of course, can be obtained almost for the asking to fit any objective. In many instances the so-called "news" is molded and fitted to supply what the writer or the "service" believes the subscribers desire to read. These pseudo-news sources do little real harm, however, for they entertain and amuse some of their readers, please others, and are generally appraised as having little value so far as really affecting public opinion is concerned. With this general estimate, bona fide newspaper reporters and correspondents agree. . . . *The Public Papers and Addresses of Franklin D. Roosevelt,* With a Special Introduction and Explanatory Notes by President Roosevelt, New York; Random House, 1938 (Vols. I-V, for the years 1928-1932, 1933, 1934, 1935, 1936), and Macmillan, 1941 (Vols. VI-IX, for the years 1937, 1938, 1939, 1940), Vol. II, Note following Item 9, p. 38. To the same effect, see *ibid.* Vol. IV, Item 188, p. 512; *ibid.,* Vol. VII, Item 54, pp. 278-280. See also Walter Davenport, "The President and The Press," *Collier's,* Vol. 115, No. 4, p. 12, January 27, 1945.)

Comment on Editorial Comment:

A short while ago, Mr. Roosevelt's press secretary, Stephen T. Early, told reporters that FDR had known exactly what he wanted to do after he left the White House. The subject of more newspaper editorials perhaps than any other man in history, Mr. Roosevelt wanted to publish a tabloid-size newspaper having no editorial comment. "He believed that if the people were given the facts," said Steve Early, "they could draw their own conclusions." (*Time,* Vol. XLVI, No. 9, p. 56, August 27, 1945.)

The following excerpt from the transcript of a Press Conference, April 21, 1938, elaborates on FDR's views on this subject:

THE PRESIDENT: . . . I will tell you a story: A year and a half ago, when John Boettiger went out to take charge of the Seattle *Post-Intelligencer,* we all knew he had a hot potato. In the first place, he had a paper that ran between three and four hundred thousand dollars a year in the red. That is no joke. In the second place, he had old man Hearst as a boss, which is no joke either. *(Laughter)*

However, he had got a pretty good understanding out of the old man, Hearst, that he would not have to run these box editorials that Hearst wrote. Well, that was something. (Laughter) That was a gain. Then, in addition to that, he was going to a city that has had more violent labor troubles than almost any other city in this country.

He said, "What would you do?" I said, "Two pieces of advice from a student of publicity. Eliminate your editorial page altogether. Nobody reads it."

Now, that is horrid for me to say that to you. Mr. Ochs told me a great many years ago—not so many, about four or five years ago—that in his judgment only eight per cent of the readers of the New York *Times* read any of the editorials, and less than half of one per cent read one editorial all the way through. Now, that is Mr. Ochs.

So, I said, "John, cut out your editorial page entirely. Run some features on it, run some cartoons on it, run letters to the editor on it and clip editorials that appeal to you from other papers or weeklies or monthly magazines." *(Laughter)*

I said, "Number 2: On your news stories. You are a newspaper. You are in a labor dispute town. The next time you have a strike down on the water front, take two of your best men and say to Mr. A, 'You go down and you cover the water-front story for tomorrow's papers and you get in your story, the story of the strikers from their point of view, and write your lead that the strikers claimed yesterday that so and so and so and so, and that the leader of the strikers, Bridges' man, said so and so and so and so.'

"And then say to Mr. B, 'You go down there and you write your story from the point of view of the shippers, the owners of the freight that is tied up, and you write your lead that yesterday on the water front the shippers and the shipowners claimed the following.' You run those two stories in parallel columns on the front page, and do not make them too long, so that the reading public will get both sides at the same time."

Q. Did he follow your suggestion, sir?

THE PRESIDENT: He did not. (Laughter)

Q. Has he made a big success of his paper?

THE PRESIDENT: He is in the black, probably because he did not take my advice. But I will say this, that he did honest reporting.

Q. That was good advice, Mr. President.

THE PRESIDENT: You think it was good advice? Well, anyway he got in the black and that is the main thing. (The Public Papers and Addresses of Franklin D. Roosevelt, Vol. VII, Item 54, pp. 293-295.)

FDR on Unnecessary Excrescences:

Despite the fact that this volume shows FDR as a columnist—and unpaid in the bargain—it is questionable whether he would have taken up his pen again for this purpose. In December 1944 he observed during a press conference that newspaper columnists had become an "unnecessary excrescence on our civilization." (The New York Times, December 23, 1944, p. 1; see also comment of Arthur Krock, the N. Y. Times, December 28, 1945, p. 18.) The same thinking by FDR was earlier (1938) reflected when he stated:

People like to read the Walter Winchells and the Paul Mallons and the other columns; they like to read the amusing stories, the Pearson and Allen stuff, and so forth and so on. But in the long run, they are getting to the point of saying, "Oh, it is funny, it is grand; I love to read it every morning but what can I believe? I have read so much of this sort of stuff now for years and years." (The Public Papers and Addresses of Franklin D. Roosevelt, Vol. VII, Item 54, pp. 282-283.)

WARM SPRINGS

Beginnings:

"According to historical records the first white settlers pushed westward from the east coast of Georgia, reaching the warm springs shortly after 1825. Until the early 1840's Warm Springs was a post tavern on the military highway leading to Columbus, Georgia.

"The comparatively cool climate and the remarkable pool of warm water soon made the place a favorite summer resort. People from the coastal plain, the hot lowlands, sought the cool breezes of Warm Springs, and it became a noted carriage resort for the well-to-do people of that area.

"In the early days, the warm water of the pool was piped into a number of small tanks or bathing tubs, and those who visited at the Meriwether Inn (demolished in 1934 to make way for Georgia Hall) bathed in these separate tiny pools.

"Until the advent of the automobile, guests of Warm Springs were driven in state in a deluxe stage coach over a six mile scenic route from the railroad station to the Inn, although the station was but a half mile away by direct route.

"As the automobile gradually came into favor and people could travel greater distances more rapidly, Warm Springs declined in popularity as a resort. It was rather neglected, in fact, when in 1924 the possibilities of the natural facilities at Warm Springs, Georgia, for the hydrotherapeutic treatment of the after-effects of infantile paralysis were brought to the attention of the Honorable Franklin D. Roosevelt . . ." (*Georgia Warm Springs Foundation: Annual Report For the Fiscal Year Ended September 30, 1941, p. 11.* This report has a foreword by Mr. Roosevelt—one of his little known writings.)

The correspondence between Loyless and Roosevelt:
To date, only one of Mr. Roosevelt's biographers has shed much light on the relationship of Loyless and FDR. Earle Looker, *This Man Roosevelt,* New York: Brewer, Warren & Putnam, 1932, pp. 118-130, tells a large part of the story. With the exception of confusion in some of the dates and the portrayal of Tom Loyless as much older than he actually was, the record presented is accurate and illuminating. Very valuable is the correspondence between FDR and TWL, to which Mr. Roosevelt gave Mr. Looker access and which was first published in *This Man Roosevelt.* While such correspondence will be available at the Franklin D. Roosevelt Library, the present writer is indebted to Mr. Looker for the liberal use made of it. Mr. Looker writes (p. 118):

> I had access to the facts. Franklin Roosevelt's personal files from 1924 to 1926 were handed over intact to me; no selection was made; no records were removed.

SDR on TWL and FDR:
In her little book of intimate reminiscence, the President's mother writes:

> Together they pored over the plans for the development of Warm Springs, but long before it assumed anything like the proportions it did in later years, Mr. Loyless, who at that time was writing a column for a Macon paper, was taken very ill and had to abandon his work. Franklin took over the writing of his column and from all accounts did

a creditable job, for Tom Loyless held the assignment until the day of his death. *(My Boy Franklin,* as told by Mrs. James Roosevelt to Isabel Leighton and Gabrielle Forbush, New York: Ray Long & Richard R. Smith, 1933, p. 104.)

George Foster Peabody:

Born in Columbus, Georgia, July 27, 1852, George Foster Peabody was educated in private schools in Columbus and in Connecticut; he did not attend college. His business career began in 1866 in a wholesale dry goods commission firm in New York. He followed this line until 1880, when he became associated with Spencer Trask, a New York banker. As a banker, Mr. Peabody was especially active in the direction of railway and electrical development projects, and he accumulated substantial railway, timber, mining, coal and coke interests in this country and in Mexico. Retiring from business in 1906, he continued many other interests. Throughout his life Mr. Peabody was a close observer of current political and financial affairs. In 1880, he was treasurer of the American Free Trade League, and from 1895 on, he advocated a single tax on land values, government ownership of railroads and public franchise corporations. In politics, he was a Democrat, serving as Treasurer of the Democratic National Committee from 1896 to 1905. He was also active in national and state civil service reform associations and in several educational, religious and philanthropic organizations. In 1910, Governor Hughes of New York appointed him Chairman of the New York State Reservation Commission at Saratoga Springs. Under his direction, Saratoga was completely transformed, misuse of the springs was stopped, and the curative waters were permitted to flow freely. He retired from this position in 1915, serving in a like capacity however, in 1930, during Mr. Roosevelt's Governorship. Mr. Peabody served as Deputy Chairman of the Federal Reserve Bank of New York, 1914 through 1921. While Mr. Peabody did not attend college, he held honorary degrees from several institutions including an A.M. from Harvard in 1903, and an LL.D. from Washington and Lee University, 1903, and from the University of Georgia, 1906, and others. A bachelor, Mr. Peabody had a winter home at Warm Springs known as "Pine Glade," and it was there that he died on March 4, 1938. (See *The National Cyclopedia of American Biography,* Vol. XV, p. 140, 1916, and *Who's Who in America,* 1936-1937, Vol. 19, p. 1912.)

Major Cohen:

John S. Cohen was born in 1870. He commanded the Third Georgia U. S. Volunteers Infantry in the Spanish-American War. A special writer on politics and a former Washington correspondent, he was well acquainted in political circles. From 1917, he was editor and publisher of the Atlanta *Journal;* from 1924 to 1932 he was a member of the Democratic National Committee, at one time serving as Vice-Chairman. In 1932, Major Cohen was appointed United States Senator from Georgia to fill out the term of Senator William Harris who died. The Major died in 1935. (See the New York *Times,* May 14, 1935, p. 21.)

The Thanksgiving at Warm Springs:

It was Mr. Roosevelt's custom, even after he became President, to have his Thanksgiving dinner at Georgia Hall with the people being treated at Warm Springs. When dinner was over, he usually reminisced with them about the early days, and these talks are among the choice reading in his *Public Papers.* The portions the editor has taken to describe FDR's reactions on his first visit are from Volume IV, Item 175, p. 479; Volume VII, Item 151, p. 611; Volume III, Item 189, p. 487.

Gregory's Interview With Mr. Roosevelt:

The Atlanta *Journal* account of Mr. Roosevelt's first visit to Warm Springs was to a very large extent responsible for the attraction of infantile paralysis victims to that place. The contents of that article, however, have been handled only sketchily by Mr. Roosevelt's chief biographers to date (Looker, *This Man Roose-*

velt, p. 123, and Lindley, *Franklin D. Roosevelt: A Career in Progressive Democracy,* Indianapolis: Bobbs Merrill, 1931, pp. 209-10). Looker and Lindley are considered "chief" in the sense that they were early and have been widely copied on such matters as Gregory's interview. Most accounts of the interview state that Mr. Roosevelt was pictured with Annette Kellerman and their recovery from infantile paralysis is said to have been contrasted in the story; whereas, as a matter of fact, FDR often laughed at the coincidence of his being pictured in a bathing suit in Gregory's story, while on an opposite page was a picture of Annette Kellerman, also in a bathing suit, illustrating an advertisement of some sort. It was always the contrast in figures that appealed to Roosevelt's sense of humor. Annette Kellerman played no part in Gregory's story.

Because of the importance of this story in the history of Warm Springs and because of the inadequacy of its treatment thus far, the entire text as it appeared in the Atlanta *Journal* is printed here (see Mr. Roosevelt's own comment on page 27 of this book):

> Franklin D. Roosevelt, New York lawyer and banker, assistant secretary of the navy during the World War, and Democratic nominee for vice president in 1920, is literally swimming himself back to health and strength at Warm Springs, Ga.
>
> A graduate of Harvard and Columbia universities, an athlete of note in both Alma Maters, an outdoor lover from his boyhood, fond of nature, of boys, and of boys' affairs, Mr. Roosevelt was of strong physique and great endurance until he was stricken during the infantile paralysis epidemic in New York in the year of 1921. In fact, he had answered the call of the wild, as was his wont, before his illness, and was at a hunting lodge in the Maine woods when the paralysis struck him.
>
> Mr. Roosevelt does not know how he contracted the dread disease, and does not regard himself as more outstanding or unfortunate than the hundreds of other adults

who became victims at the same time by the disease usually confined to childhood. All he does know is that he was hit, and hit hard, with the result that both of his legs were immovable for many months. Gradually he acquired the skill necessary to drag himself around on crutches, and, undaunted, he was a predominant figure in the Democratic national convention in New York last June, making a memorable address in placing the name of Governor Al Smith before the delegates as a presidential candidate.

It was a sort of coincidence that brought Warm Springs, Ga., to Mr. Roosevelt's attention. Three years ago Louis Joseph, a New Yorker who formerly lived at Columbus, hit upon the idea of trying Warm Springs as the locale for a fight against the effects of infantile paralysis. He was in far worse shape than Mr. Roosevelt, it is said, but he bathed persistently in the waters of Warm Springs, where the pool has a natural temperature of 90 degrees the year around.

Mr. Joseph derived remarkable benefit from the springs, and spent the entire summer there. The next year he was on hand when the hotel season opened, and was still there when the hostelry closed its doors. Last summer he was back again, so greatly improved that he was able to attend to the duties of hotel clerk, and to lead dances in the pavilion on several occasions.

Tom Loyless, former Augusta and Columbus newspaper publisher, who is now in charge of the development of the Warm Springs properties, casually mentioned the case of Mr. Joseph to George Foster Peabody, New York philanthropist who is associated in the Warm Springs enterprises.

"That gives me an idea. I'll get my friend Franklin Roosevelt down here, if I can," Mr. Peabody exclaimed.

Mr. Loyless was in New York recently, and Mr. Peabody arranged for an interview between Mr. Roosevelt and Mr. Loyless. The result was that Mr. Roosevelt rented a cottage at Warm Springs, and arrived there on October 3 to give the baths a try-out.

Mr. Roosevelt and Mr. Loyless, in adjoining cottages, are the only residents of the dozen or more small houses surrounding the Warm Springs hotel at the present time. The hotel has closed for the winter season. Mr. Loyless is acting as official host to Mr. Roosevelt, and is giving him the run of the reserve, and of several counties.

The distinguished visitor has the large swimming pool all to himself for two hours or more each day. He swims, dives, uses the swinging rings and horizontal bar over the water, and finally crawls out on the concrete pier for a sun bath that lasts another hour. Then he dresses, has lunch, rests a bit on a delightfully shady porch, and spends the afternoon driving over the surrounding country, in which he is intensely interested.

Not only are the swims and the sun baths delightful innovations to Mr. Roosevelt, but his method of living is enchanting, he admits. Living a full half mile from the town of Warm Springs, formerly known as Bullochville, he is protected from the intrusion of the curious, and is even favored by infrequent mail deliveries. He expressed real relief at being two or three days behind on the news of the world.

"Has the ZR-3 landed?" he asked eagerly, on Thursday afternoon, October 16, and was surprised to learn that the great Zeppelin had been in its moorings a day and a half.

"I am deriving wonderful benefit from my stay here," Mr. Roosevelt said. "This place is great. See that right leg? It's the first time I have been able to move it at all in three years."

Mr. Roosevelt does not attribute any medicinal effects to the Warm Springs water, but he gives the water credit for his ability to remain in it two hours or more, without tiring in the least, and the rest of the credit for his improvement is given to Georgia's sunshine.

"The best infantile paralysis specialist in New York told me that the only way to overcome the effects of the disease was to swim as much as possible, and bask in the sunlight. Conditions here are ideal for both prescriptions. The water in some way relaxes muscles drawn taut by the disease, and gives the limbs much greater action. The sunshine has curative effects, I understand."

So marked have the benefits been in his case, Mr. Roosevelt plans to return to Warm Springs in March or April to remain two or three months. At that time he will build a cottage on the hilltop, so that he may spend a portion of each year there until he is completely cured. Even then he plans to keep coming back, as he likes Georgia and Georgians, he remarked.

Nobody can explain just why the waters of Warm Springs flowing from the foot of Pine Mountain are almost as warm as the average person's blood. Nor can anyone explain why the waters on the other side of the mountain, where the United States fish hatcheries are located, are unnaturally cold.

Mr. Roosevelt made no effort to explain the phenomenon, but he did remark, "Poor fish," with a characteristic grin.

George Foster Peabody, his nephew, Charles Peabody, a noted New York architect, and Mr. Loyless have enlarged and rebuilt the open-air swimming pool at Warm Springs, and are now at work remodeling four inclosed swimming pools on the hotel grounds. They are planning extensive developments there, with the possible expenditure of several million dollars, in the erection of a new hotel that will be made a year-round health resort. A golf course has already been built, and other improvements are under way.

Mr. Roosevelt has made a great hit with the people of Warm Springs who have met him, and they are extending him a hearty welcome as a prospective regular visitor. A number of Georgia's public men have also called to pay their respects and extend greetings. Georgians who attended the Democratic national convention have been especially cordial, because they appreciate the interest Mr. Roosevelt showed in them, and his courtesy in apologizing, as an Al Smith leader, for unfortunate and embarrassing incidents in connection with the convention.

"Say! Let's get one of the hot dogs this man makes just outside the swimming pool. They're great," Mr. Roosevelt challenged. With him everything in Warm Springs is "Great" or "Fine" or "Wonderful." That is the spirit that has carried him to remarkable heights for a man just past his fortieth year, and it is the spirit that is going to restore him to his pristine health and vigor, for political and financial battles and successes in the years that are to come.

The Effort for "Common Counsel":

The important facts in FDR's attempt to harmonize the Democrats in 1924-1925 can be found in the New York *Times,* March 9, 1925, p. 1; March 10, 1925, p. 20; April 5, 1925, p. 5; and April 10, 1925, p. 18.

Intramural Activities, 1924-1925:

Two news items reveal that while trying during the winter 1924-1925 to reconcile his fellow Democrats, FDR was also sorting out his collection of naval prints. It was reported (the New York *Times,* January 4, 1925, II p. 4) in a story headed "Naval Prints on Sale":

> Franklin D. Roosevelt is putting on the market many early American and English historic naval and marine prints and paintings and also several experimental naval models, and these, with the addition of some other items from other collectors, and all of which may be seen at the Anderson Galleries, are to be sold there Friday morning.
>
> The models include those of the American Line Steamship Philadelphia, fitted up for World War service as the Harrisburg; the Von Steuben, formerly the German commerce raider the Kronprinz Wilhelm, and the George Washington.
>
> There are early English, French and Dutch marine and naval prints, naval and marine printings of the American School, and early American naval and marine prints, portraits and views.

About a week later, another story (the New York *Times,* January 10, 1925, p. 2) captioned, "Marine Prints Sold" appeared:

> A sale of naval and marine prints and paintings from the collection of Franklin D. Roosevelt, former Assistant

Secretary of the Navy, brought $4,537 last evening at the
Anderson Galleries. E. F. Collins, agent, paid the highest
price, $255, for a painting by C. Fischer of the U. S. S.
Niagara, bound for Japan, and Miss H. Counihan, agent,
paid $250 for an aquatint of Philadelphia seen from
Cooper's Ferry, drawn and engraved by J. Wood.

J. D. Lyons paid $150 for a lithograph by Endicott &
Co., of New Bedford, in 1808, painted by W. A. Wall. I. S.
Olds bought an engraving by A. Lawson of a painting of
Perry's Victory on Lake Erie by T. Birch for $105. Max
Williams paid $125 for a painting by Louis Reux of the
English bark "Harry Seaman." A painting by Thomas
Birch of the full-rigged bark "Fannie M. Cavill" went on
order for $135.

Roosevelt Slept Here:

While he stayed in the MacPherson cottage on his first visit to
Warm Springs, on his second visit, when he wrote the *Telegraph*
column, FDR took the cottage of Mr. William Hart, the brother-
in-law of Leighton MacPherson. This was just "across the way"
on an eighteen foot roadway from the cottage leased by TWL for
his family's use from the Josephs, who owned several cottages at
the resort at that time.

The Circulation of the Telegraph:

In his column of April 14, 1925, introducing his substitute, Tom
Loyless, perhaps with his tongue in his cheek, places the readers of
the *Telegraph* at "a hundred thousand or so." According to *American Newspaper Annual and Directory,* Philadelphia: N. W. Ayer
& Son, Inc., 1925, the yearly average paid daily circulation of
the *Telegraph* for 1925 was 26,822, and the Sunday, 27,376. At
least it's clear that not all the readers were paying customers.

Tom Loyless on FDR's First Column:

Just below Mr. Roosevelt's first *Telegraph* column, this letter
was printed:

Warm Springs, Ga., April 13, 7 P.M.

Editor of The Telegraph: I understand from his very charming secretary that my neighbor, Hon. Franklin D. Roosevelt, following-out his promise to me the other day, dictated and put in the mail this afternoon an article that is supposed to take the place of mine for Thursday morning. Which is all right and according to agreement, except in one particular, to-wit: That I expected to see and pass on—well, anyway, the first of these articles, in order to guard against anything derogatory to myself; or in general anything that isn't quite up to the standard of my column, etc. But since it got over to the postoffice without me seeing it, and having a fair and reasonable chance to edit same, will you not, as an old friend and fellow worker in the Master's Kingdom, do me the favor to give the said Roosevelt article the once-over, and fix it up like it ought to be; being particular to see to it that nothing of a political nature creeps in. For, all along, you know, I have rather prided myself on being able to keep my column "neutral even in thought." Thanking you in advance, and trusting that everyone understands that Mr. Roosevelt and not the undersigned is now writing my column in the Telegraph for a few days or as long as he likes, and that I do not even accept the responsibility of putting his articles in the mail, I am

Sincerely yours,

Thomas W. Loyless

P.S. Also, if it isn't too much trouble, and for obvious prudential reasons, won't you kindly change the caption of my column for the time being, to—"As Roosevelt Sees It." Thanks. T.W.L.

Editorial Comment on FDR's Telegraph *Columns:*

The following editorial comment from the Dalton (Georgia) *Citizen* was printed in the *Telegraph,* May 12, 1925:

It isn't necessary for the government to be niggardly with expenditures in order to reduce taxes. But it is necessary to practice economy by cutting out all unnecessary bureaus and useless commissions. And this is what President Coolidge is striving to do.

Franklin D. Roosevelt, writing in The Macon Telegraph, points out that the government can save hundreds of thousands of dollars a year by ridding the various departments in Washington of a large number of employes whose chief occupation seems to be to kill both time and efficiency by doing as little as possible.

Go to any State capital and one is impressed with the presence of idlers on the State payrolls. What is true of the State capitals is true of the national capital. Mr. Roosevelt shows that a great saving can be made by the application of civil service rules, sensibly enforced, thus making for the advancement of the worthy employe and the elimination of the unworthy.

If a private enterprise were to adopt the extravagant plans of State and Federal government it would meet disaster in short order.

As a result of political rewards two are very frequently doing the job in State affairs that one could do better and quicker.

A weeding out process is essential to government economy and efficiency.

And it must not be forgotten that foolish, not to say silly, laws are responsible for many of the extravagant and wasteful operations that are weighing heavily on the taxpayers and crowding to an overflow the jails and penitentiaries of the country.

Another comment from the Fitzgerald (Georgia) *Leader,* clipped in the *Telegraph* for May 12, 1925:

Franklin D. Roosevelt, who is spending some time in Warm Springs in writing in The Macon Telegraph, on "Taxation in Georgia," confirms the needs of the passage of a law as advocated by the Leader for these many years past. In regard to the under-valuation of personal property for taxation in Georgia, Mr. Roosevelt says:

"I am told that very much the same situation exists in Georgia today; that, for instance, personal property (merchandise) in Atlanta alone is insured for a larger amount than the total assessed value of all the merchandise in the State of Georgia put together. If that is true, your personal property law ought to be repealed or enforced."

If Mr. Roosevelt is correctly informed, and we believe he is, a law, as advocated by this paper, to avoid all insurance policies in excess of their taxable value, in the event they become a claim on insurance companies, would force their return for taxation at their fair value. The tax rate should be lowered correspondingly, as such a practice would bring in enough money into the State or county treasuries, to defray all of the public expenses. If the State would go a step further, make the tax receipt equivalent to an insurance policy against fire, the property owners would save at least one-third or more of their cumulative payments now going for insurance and taxes to cities and counties and State.

The Columnist and His Bibliographer:

Not long ago, in appraising and cataloging the literary efforts of Franklin Roosevelt, his bibliographer (the designation is FDR's) observed: "Before his election to the Presidency, Mr. Roosevelt had no reputation as an author. For a few weeks one Spring he had written a column of news commentary for a Georgia paper and proved to himself that nobody faced with such a stint could say something worthwhile every day." (Frederick B. Adams, Jr., "Mr. Roosevelt Continues, as President and Author," *Papers of the Bibliographical Society of America,* Volume 37, p. 223, Third Quarter, 1943. For additional bibliographical data on FDR, see Mr. Adams' earlier and equally interesting and competent paper: "The President As Author," *The Colophon,* New Series, Vol. 1, No. 4, pp. 487-497, Spring, 1936.)

What They Left There:

Tom Loyless' struggle to develop Warm Springs and FDR's heroic battle there to recover from polio have left a very definite imprint on the place. " . . . That thing we call 'the spirit of Warm Springs.' " (*The Public Papers and Addresses of Franklin D. Roosevelt, op. cit.,* Vol. II, Item 170, pp. 502-504.) See also *Georgia Warm Springs Foundation: Annual Report for Fiscal Year Ended September 30, 1941,* p. 6, stating that Warm Springs "has stressed and fostered the building of as normal a social life as is possible. That this has been accomplished to a great extent is witnessed by the spirit of cheer, optimism and good fellowship among the patients, whether they be on stretchers, in hospital beds, in wheel chairs or on crutches." In this connection FDR's own account of his illness, stating his conviction that "belief on the patient's part" that he will recover is one of the major parts of treatment for infantile paralysis, was recently brought to light in a letter written by Mr. Roosevelt during his first visit to Warm Springs, dated October 11, 1924. (" 'A History of the Case' in Franklin D. Roosevelt's Own Words," *The Journal of the South Carolina Medical Association,* Vol. XLII, January 1946, p. 1.)

"When the Azaleas Were in Bloom":

The editor was thinking of Lincoln and used the phrase "when the lilacs were in bloom again" at the end of the story about Tom Loyless, FDR and Warm Springs. When the present writer's good friend, Margaret L. Suckley (a cousin of Mr. Roosevelt who was with him on the last visit to Warm Springs) read the first draft of the manuscript, she commented, "I love your last paragraph . . . could I make a slight suggestion here that you change the word 'lilacs' to 'azaleas'? Every day during those two weeks, Laura Delano and I, with her setter 'Sister' and 'Fala,' walked into the woods and came back, laden with azaleas. The house was full of them—always fresh and fragrant—FDR mentions them on April 16, 1925."

DUTCHESS COUNTY

The Hudson Valley and the American Tradition:

Shortly after Mr. Roosevelt went to the White House, *Fortune* published a very able analysis of the effect of his background on his personality and judgment. It seems worth quoting this article at some length as an excellent footnote to the Dutchess County columns:

> Mr. Roosevelt's past, personal and ancestral, is a curiously symmetrical and uncomplicated whole. It is cut from a single piece. And it has a single significance. . . . Substantially the one fact of importance about the President is the American tradition.

And the article went on to attempt a definition of its terms:

> The fact is, of course, as any traveler out of the ordinary ruts will know, that the American tradition is as distinct and peculiar as that of any country. It is however an agricultural, or rather a rural tradition. It never existed in the great cities, for the great cities were never, in any but a geographic sense, American. It was to be found only in the small communities. And it neither had nor has any relation whatever to industrialism. From the industrial point of view it is pure anachronism. For it is a tradition of individual responsibilty and its guiding principle is the principle that a man must control and direct his own life, that he must take full responsibility for the well-being of the community in which he lives, and that he cannot in decency surrender the direction of his life or of his community to any other power. It is, in other words, a tradition of indi-

vidualism. But it is not the tradition of individualism which, with the spurious addition of the word "rugged" rang through the political orations of the '90's and the 1900's. Rugged individualism is a gray horse of a very different color. It is the individualism of the so-called Empire Builders, the individualism of unlimited rights—and no obligations whatever. It is a degradation of individualism which has today brought the whole concept of individualism into disrepute. The individualism of the American tradition is a totally different thing: it is the individualism of duty. Its end is the freedom of life, not the accumulation of wealth. And its means are responsible and independent citizenship as that word has been understood for a hundred years in the American colonies and for a hundred and fifty years in the American states.

Roosevelt's background, according to the article, was typical of this pattern:

The American tradition so defined obviously exists only among a small minority of the population—the small minority of Americans of old stock who have lived for a great many generations directly upon the land. The family of the President is such a family. It is a quite undistinguished American family of Dutch origin which has lived in Dutchess County, seventy miles up the Hudson from New York, since the French and Indian wars. It is, and long has been, moderately wealthy. James Roosevelt, the President's father, served for a time as a Vice President of the Delaware & Hudson. Sara Delano, the President's mother, was the daughter of a China trader who had retired with a fortune to an estate across the river. But the whole background of the family is rural. It inherited the tradition of the families living in the Valley. It had a sense of the community. It had a habit of citizenship. It was part of the Republic. And that tradition the President quite naturally and inevitably inherited. He has always been interested in people as only a man living in a small community can be interested in people. He thinks in terms of people. He never makes an abstract decision but always a decision stated in terms of the probable effect upon one group or another. And his mental picture of the country, his primary assumption about American life, is the somewhat questionable assumption that America still is a collection, a congeries, of such small communities as he knows. He becomes almost oracular on the subject. He is certain that the country *is* just that—and that what will be good for the small communities will be good for the nation . . . ("What's to Become of Us?" *Fortune,* Vol. VIII, No. 6, p. 112, December, 1933; reprinted in *The Roosevelt Omnibus, op. cit.,* "The Enigma," at pp. 109-112.)

The Old Red Maxwell:

The story about this political chariot used by Mr. Roosevelt and his running-mates in the 1910 campaign comes from a White House letter written by FDR to Morgan Hoyt, which the latter showed the editor. It is told also in *Yank,* May 11, 1945, which, incidentally, carries an interesting article on FDR and his friends at Beacon.

What in the Name of Croker and Tweed Is He Doing Here?:

Just prior to becoming a *Standard* columnist, Mr. Roosevelt made the nominating speech for Al Smith at Houston. The following dispatch by Will Durant from the Democratic Convention was printed in the New York *World-Telegram* on June 25, 1928:

Here on the stage is Franklin Roosevelt, beyond comparison the finest man that has appeared at either convention; beside him the master minds who held the platform at Kansas City where crude bourgeois, porters suddenly made rich.

A figure tall and proud even in suffering; a face of classic profile; pale with years of struggle against paralysis; a frame nervous and yet self-controlled with that tense, taut unity of spirit which lifts the complex soul above those whose calmness is only a stolidity; most obviously a gentleman and a scholar. A man softened and cleansed and illumined with pain. What in the name of Croker and Tweed is he doing here?

Nothing better could be said for the Governor of New York than that Franklin Roosevelt loves him. See how one mind and one heart have won the affectionate admiration of scientists and ward-heelers, students and wire-pullers, social workers and ballot-box stuffers, philosophers and pugilists. Perhaps there is something in this man Smith after all? Hear the nominating speech: it is not a battery of rockets, bombs and tear-drawing gas—it is not shouted, it is quietly read; there is hardly a gesture, hardly a raising of the voice. This is a civilized man; he could look Balfour and Poincaré in the face. For the moment we are lifted up.

Ed Hayden Reminisces:

Once a newspaperman always a newspaperman. In 1945, Mr. Hayden wrote his recollections of FDR for his present employer. Although a bit inaccurate on detail, the broad lines of the part of his story regarding the column "Between Neighbors" are interesting. This appeared in the Newburgh News, April 13, 1945, p. 2:

In 1928 there were many hot issues, but the question of repeal of the 18th Amendment transcended all others. With typical Roosevelt political intuition the Squire of Hyde Park planned a pre-election denunciation of the law as a means of capitalizing on the wave of opposition to the measure which President Herbert Hoover described as a "noble experiment."

Foreseeing developments of great importance to the people of the nation, Mr. Roosevelt decided to become a columnist. He arranged with the writer, then editor of the Beacon Light in Beacon, to write a weekly column on matters of national import.

Under a two-column head, "Our Neighbor," Mr. Roosevelt wrote one week on agricultural problems, the next week on transportation, and continued for four weeks on other national issues, with the announced intention of

173

devoting the column just prior to the 1928 election to the Prohibition issue.

The column was being syndicated weekly to large, medium and small newspapers from coast to coast. The clientele was growing rapidly, indicating the importance which editors throughout the country attached to statements made by Mr. Roosevelt. However, Mr. Roosevelt's career as a Columnist on a small weekly newspaper was short lived.

One day Mr. Roosevelt's secretary, the late Margaret LeHand, known to him as "Missy," called the editor to announce that Mr. Roosevelt would not be able to continue the column because of unforeseen circumstances. Mr. Roosevelt later made known that Gov. Alfred E. Smith had asked him to run for Governor to bolster Smith's chances of carrying New York State in the Presidential race.

Mr. Roosevelt said he had agreed to go on a stumping tour upstate, which would make it impossible for him to continue his writings. However, he expressed complete satisfaction with the reactions from widespread publication of his articles.

An additional account of the relationship of FDR, Hayden and the *Standard* appeared in the *Gannetteer* (a publication for employees of the Gannett newspapers) June, 1945, p. 12, entitled "Newburgh News Man Once FDR's 'Boss' "; it read as follows:

In 1928 Franklin D. Roosevelt was columnist on a Beacon weekly—an "employe" of Publisher Ed Hayden, who's now a Newburgh News staffer. Hayden told about it in The News the day after President Roosevelt died.

Ed recalled that Private Citizen Roosevelt had eyes on the White House, even in 1928, when FDR used his neighbors as a sounding board of opinion. Hyde Park and Beacon are in Dutchess County.

The President-to-be recognized the value of newspaper publicity, Hayden noted. And to keep in the national spotlight, Mr. Roosevelt consented to write one article a week for the Beacon Light. Understanding: Ed would syndicate the column.

For four Monday mornings then Publisher Hayden visited the big Hyde Park mansion. He'd get his copy—usually three or four typewritten pages—would chat with the columnist, would decline Mr. Roosevelt's request for criticism, then would scurry back to Beacon to have the column set 8 pt. d. c. Boxed head of the Page 1 feature: "Our Neighbor."

Galley proofs went to 300 selected newspapers, along with the announcement that rates depended on circulations. Many metropolitan papers bought the feature; Entrepreneur Hayden thought he'd tapped a coast-to-coast gold mine.

The Roosevelt columnist B. E. (before Eleanor) discussed agriculture the first week; transportation the second. But the service expired after the fourth week: Mr. Roosevelt had yielded to Al Smith's request that he seek election as governor—to bolster Al's chances of getting New York's presidential vote.

FDR received no pay for his weekly stint. All profits went to Hayden, and they were increasing fabulously. Termination of the deal hit hard at the small weekly's delicate box office.

But 14 years later FDR again tossed "easy money" into Hayden's lap. The former syndicateer responded to a greeting from Mr. Roosevelt in the summer of 1942; served in the Air Corps for a year; this time he got $54 "easy money" a month.

Comment in the Times:

The New York *Times,* August 3, 1928, p. 38, stated in part: "Will Rogers and other metropolitan columnists are warned by Franklin D. Roosevelt to look out for their laurels, as he has joined the staff of The Beacon Standard, Dutchess County weekly newspaper, contributing a series of articles entitled 'Between Neighbors.' In the first of the series, in which Mr. Roosevelt will discuss topics of interest to the people of his home county, he comments upon the recent visit of Senator Heflin of Alabama to Dutchess County, and also discusses the effect of present newspaper policies."

And in the Standard:

An editorial entitled "Mr. Roosevelt's Articles" appeared in the *Standard,* September 13, 1928:

> The articles which are being exclusively run in the Standard from the pen of Franklin D. Roosevelt, continue to attract much attention throughout the country. The Standard is furnishing these articles to a number of papers in the South and far West and every mail brings subscriptions to run during the course of Mr. Roosevelt's articles.
>
> He is a writer of keen ability and has the faculty of putting his theories clearly and concisely. While there is some attempt to answer them, the replies seem not to reply but to quibble.

"Address Me There If Anything Turns Up":

With regard to the message written by FDR to Morgan Hoyt at the time Mr. Roosevelt went to Warm Springs in September, 1928, it is Mr. Hoyt's recollection that it was merely a note clipped to the column dated September 15, 1928, when it was prepared for the *Standard.* However, the message has the appearance of being more than a note as there is an indication the top has been torn off. It is possible there was an address or additional writing above that which is given here. That is, what we have here may be merely a portion of a letter, the remainder of which has been destroyed. Morgan Hoyt very generously supplied the editor with a photostat of the note and permitted the use of its contents in this book.

Torchlight at Hyde Park:

Election Night, 1944, was the last time Mr. Roosevelt talked with most of his Dutchess County neighbors. As usual, they came by torchlight to the "big house" to congratulate him on another victory. The gracious lady who wrote the Foreword for this book describes the picture (*My Day,* Nov. 8, 1944):

> More people than ever came down from Hyde Park with flares and a band, led by Moses Smith and Elmer Van Wagner, who is the Democratic supervisor in our district. They always report apologetically that "The President has carried his own district by a few votes, but lost the town of Hyde Park." "Nevertheless," they said, "in spite of the fact that they vote against him, all his neighbors love him." This little speech always amuses me, for it seems to me that they must vote as a tradition, but hope to be beaten—which doesn't make any real sense.

ACKNOWLEDGMENTS

In the preparation of this book, I have been aided most generously by several persons, and it is a pleasure to make certain acknowledgments. Miss Margaret L. Suckley of the Franklin D. Roosevelt Library, Hyde Park, New York, was most cooperative and generous in her assistance; Miss Florence M. Gifford, Head of the General Reference Division, Cleveland Public Library, Cleveland, Ohio; Mrs. James E. Powers, Librarian, Washington Memorial Library, Macon, Georgia; Miss Bessie B. Gilchrist, Librarian, Young Men's Library Association, Augusta, Georgia; and Miss Marion Davies, Librarian, Howland Circulating Library, Beacon, New York, each undertook extensive research in my behalf, and this note of acknowledgment is far from adequate recognition of their services. Mr. Loyless' daughter, Mrs. Patrick H. Mell of Wayne, Pennsylvania, and his brothers-in-law, Mr. A. M. Kennedy, Atlanta, and Mr. W. F. Kennedy of Augusta, Georgia, graciously wrote me at considerable length their personal recollections of Mr. Loyless. Mr. Cleburne E. Gregory, political editor of the Atlanta *Journal*, gave me sidelights on his interview with Mr. Roosevelt at Warm Springs in 1924. Mr. Edward T. Hayden of Poughkeepsie, New York, supplied me much information about the *Standard* during the time he served as reporter and publisher. Mr. Morgan H. Hoyt of Albany, New York, gave me his many intimate recollections of Mr. Roosevelt and Dutchess County politics since 1910; Mr. Hoyt also generously allowed me to read his numerous personal letters from FDR—letters dating from 1913 to the day Mr. Roosevelt returned from Yalta. Mr. W. T. Anderson, editor and chairman of the Board of Directors of The Macon Telegraph Publishing Company and Mr. Robert C. Pendell, editor and publisher of the *Beacon Light and Fishkill Standard,* kindly permitted the reprinting of Mr. Roosevelt's columns which were originally published in the Macon *Daily Telegraph* and the *Standard*. Many of the paragraphs bear the expert touch of Mr. Henry Rago. Sallie T. Frisch and Ruth A. Clark bore the brunt of the stenographic and copy work necessary to complete the manuscript. It is a special pleasure to thank Mr. John Valentine, a fellow FDR collector, and his partner at The Abraham Lincoln Book Shop, Mr. Ralph Newman, for their unbounded enthusiasm and encouragement in the preparation of this book.

I am indebted also to numerous editors, writers and others for assistance and permission to quote from source materials and commentaries at considerable length:

To Mr. Jonathan Daniels and the editors of *The Saturday Evening Post* for quotations from the article, "What I Learned About Washington"; to Mr. L. C. Rosten and Harcourt, Brace & Co. for quotations from *The Washington Correspondents;* to Mr. Earle Looker for quotations from *This Man Roosevelt;* to Mr. Frederick B. Adams, Jr. and the Bibliographical Society of America, for quotations from *Papers of the Bibliographical Society of America;* to Mr. Samuel Rosenman, Random House, and The Macmillan Company for quotations from *The Public Papers and Addresses of Franklin D. Roosevelt;* to Georgia Warm Springs Foundation for permission to quote from its annual report for the fiscal year ended September 30, 1941; and to the editors of *Fortune, Time, Collier's, The American Mercury,* the New York *Times,* the New York *World Telegram,* the Newburgh *News,* the Atlanta *Journal,* and *The Gannetteer,* for quotations from their magazines and newspapers; to United Feature Syndicate for quotations from "My Day"; to Blasingame's Photo Service, Atlanta, Georgia, for the frontispiece; to Mr. Carl Faunce, Beacon, New York for photograph of *Standard* page; to Mr. Walter Morgan Pharr of Macon, Georgia for photograph of *Daily Telegraph* page; to Acme Newspictures for the photo of Mr. Roosevelt nominating Al Smith; to the Estate of Franklin D .Roosevelt; and lastly, but certainly not least, to the Franklin D. Roosevelt Library, and its director, Fred W. Shipman.

D.S.C.